Profitable Wonders

Helen Oppenheimer is a graduate of Lady Margaret Hall, Oxford, and holds a Lambeth DD. She is a former President of the Society for the Study of Christian Ethics. She writes and lectures on a range of questions in ethics and philosophical theology and has served on several Anglican commissions. Her previous titles include *The Hope of Happiness*, *Finding and Following* and *Making Good*, all published by SCM Press.

Profitable Wonders

Collected by
Helen Oppenheimer

An empty Book is like an infants Soul, in which any Thing may be written. It is Capable of all Things, but containeth Nothing. I have a Mind to fill this with Profitable Wonders.

Thomas Traherne, Centuries, I.1

scm press

British Library Cataloguing in Publication data

A catalogue record for this book is available
from the British Library

0 334 02924 4

First published in 2003 by SCM Press
9–17 St Albans Place, London N1 0NX

www.scm-canterburypress.co.uk

SCM Press is a division of
SCM-Canterbury Press Ltd

Typeset in Scala by Regent Typesetting, London
Printed and bound in Great Britain by
Creative Print and Design, Wales

In memory of my grandmother Harriet Jane Findlay,
who encouraged me to enjoy poetry.

Contents

Preface

Profitable Wonders began as a commonplace book for my own enjoyment and convenience. It turned into an anthology which has become an exploration of what I believe. Sixty years ago, as a schoolgirl, I used to copy out pieces of poetry and prose and learn some of them by heart. I did not take great heed then of exact references, innocently supposing that I could always ask my teachers for the sources. The higgledy piggledy collection began to take shape much later, when I first read Thomas Traherne and thought what a good title his phrase 'profitable wonders' would make. Some pieces have found their way into the collection by roundabout routes, which I hope will excuse the somewhat variable character of the Bibliography.

When I began to put the material into order, I found that it grouped itself in manageable sections. Palgrave in his *Golden Treasury* put his chosen poems into 'the most poetically effective order'. Less ambitiously, I have tried to set out a discernible line of thought. Assembling it has been an enjoyable and indeed a self-indulgent hobby. My excuse for not repressing its idiosyncrasy is that some people enjoy other people's eccentricities and may indeed share them. I have taken snippets which make a particular point, or whole pieces, as I felt inclined. I see a difference, though a fine one, between positively choosing parts of a longer piece, and merely setting about shortening it. I have done the former with enthusiasm and the latter only seldom and reluctantly.

Some of the pieces are serious and some more light-hearted. Some of them are more wonderful and some more profitable, but most have something of both wonder and profit about them. Each one says something which matters to me. Taken all together they express my creed in other people's words. I thought at first to let the pieces stand on their own feet without further comment; but have come to think that some signposts at the beginnings of the sections would be more considerate to anyone who would like to follow the intended direction.

The book which this has become is addressed to Christians and fringe believers. I hope it may appeal to people who mind about language and thrive on words. I was once affronted by the phrase in a church newspaper 'the scholar alone in his book-lined study'. On the contrary, the books on one's shelves are continual company, whom one can invite other people to meet, making introductions across the centuries.

A work like this owes more gratitude than can be adequately recognized. It makes one conscious of belonging to the Communion of Saints, compassed about by a great crowd of witnesses. Protestants caricature Catholics as worshipping saints and Catholics caricature Protestants as neglecting them, but what we rightly owe to fellow Christians and honoured teachers of earlier times is attentive appreciation. Apart from the Psalmists and St Paul, the mentors to whom I am conscious of owing most are Augustine of Hippo, Julian of Norwich, Thomas Traherne, Robert Browning, Edwin Muir, C. S. Lewis and Austin Farrer.

Thanks to contemporaries who have helped are more easily conveyed: to Dr Eric James for kind encouragement; to Miss Jenny Gruchy for patient accurate typing at an early stage; to Mr Donald Whitton for linguistic help with Abelard's 'O quanta qualia'; to Dr Malcolm Weisman who advised me about the Hebrew wedding blessings; to Mrs Margaret Croft who found and looked up the Oxford Hymn Book for me; to my son-in-law Ivo Mosley for advice over translations and permissions, from his experience in compiling anthologies; and once again to my husband, this time particularly for help in wrestling with software.

[x]

Preface

I have included small pieces in French, German, Italian and Latin, and one verse from the New Testament in Greek. As I am no linguist or poet I have used other people's translations when I could; but when nothing suitable was readily available I have impertinently tried to provide some idea of the meaning.

For the Bible, I have most often used the Revised Standard Version. This choice represents a compromise, an attempt to reckon with the obscurity of ancient well-loved language as it recedes into the past, without being defeated by the awkwardness which besets twenty-first century attempts at clarity. St Paul's 'brethren' included sisters, but to insist that he must always say so becomes heavy handed. Where the long-familiar words are part of the purpose of choosing a passage, and especially when they translate a poem, I have used the King James Version and indicated this; and for the same reason I have preferred Coverdale's version in the Book of Common Prayer for the Psalms.

Faith: its difficulty and possibility

For some of us, the difficulty of faith is evident and its possibility is what has to be discovered. This sequence can be more promising than starting with uncritical faith and then putting it at the mercy of growing sophistication. To go through doubt and arrive at faith is one kind of integrity which many good Christians exemplify. Some of them are represented here, along with some variegated others who shed light on faith positively or negatively.

Turn to me and be saved, all the ends of the earth! For I am God, and there is no other.

Isaiah 45.22 (Deutero-Isaiah)

Shadrach, Meshach and Abednego answered the king, O Nebuchadnezzar, we have no need to answer you in this matter. If it be so, our God whom we serve is able to deliver us from the burning fiery furnace; and he will deliver us out of your hand, O king. But if not, be it known to you, O king, that we will not serve your gods, nor worship the golden image which you have set up.

Daniel 3.16–18

Always be prepared to make a defence to anyone who calls you to account for the hope that is in you, yet do it with gentleness and reverence.

The First Epistle of St Peter 3.15

We shall trust him, if he exists, but we can hardly trust him to exist. We must have reason to think that he does.

Austin Farrer, *A Science of God?*, p. 10

Only today I have found a passage in a Christian writer where he recommends his own version of Christianity on the ground that 'only such a faith can outlast the death of old cultures and the birth of new civilisations'. You see the little rift? 'Believe this, not because it is true, but for some other reason.'

C. S. Lewis, *The Screwtape Letters*, 23

Sir, the pretending to extraordinary revelations and gifts of the Holy Ghost is a horrid thing, a very horrid thing.

Joseph Butler, To John Wesley

I should like to say at once that it will not do to put the complainants off with a merely 'clever' rejoinder, which admits of no answer but produces no conviction. If the critics have not stated their own case properly (and I think that in some respects they have not) it is our business to state it better. If it appears to us that the demands which they make upon us are nonsensical as they stand, we must try to re-formulate them in a way which does make sense. Then, but not before, we may express our disagreement with them.

H. H. Price, *Clarity Is Not Enough*, p. 16

Faith

Bolingbroke: O! who can hold a fire in his hand
              By thinking on the frosty Caucasus?
              Or cloy the hungry edge of appetite
              By bare imagination of a feast?
              Or wallow naked in December snow
              By thinking on fantastic summer's heat?

William Shakespeare, *Richard II*, I.4

Everything is what it is, and not another thing.

Joseph Butler, *Fifteen Sermons preached at the Rolls Chapel*, Preface

Glendower: I can call spirits from the vasty deep.
Hotspur: Why, so can I, and so can any man;
            But will they come when you do call for them?

William Shakespeare, *Henry IV Part I*, III.1

The sea is calm tonight,
The tide is full, the moon lies fair
Upon the Straits; – on the French coast, the light
Gleams and is gone; the cliffs of England stand,
Glimmering and vast, out in the tranquil bay.
Come to the window, sweet is the night air!
Only, from the long line of spray
Where the ebb meets the moon-blanch'd sand,
Listen! you hear the grating roar
Of pebbles which the waves suck back and fling
At their return, up the high strand,
Begin, and cease, and then again begin,
With tremulous cadence slow, and bring
The eternal note of sadness in.

Sophocles long ago
Heard it on the Aegaean, and it brought
Into his mind the turbid ebb and flow
Of human misery; we
Find also in the sound a thought,
Hearing it by this distant northern sea.

The sea of faith
Was once, too, at the full, and round earth's shore
Lay like the folds of a bright girdle furl'd;
But now I only hear
Its melancholy, long, withdrawing roar,
Retreating to the breath
Of the night-wind down the vast edges drear
And naked shingles of the world.

Ah, love, let us be true
To one another! For the world which seems
To lie before us like a land of dreams,
So various, so beautiful, so new,
Hath really neither joy, nor love, nor light,
Nor certitude, nor peace, nor help for pain;
And we are here as on a darkling plain
Swept with confused alarms of struggle and flight,
Where ignorant armies clash by night.

Matthew Arnold, 'Dover Beach'

I had become a puzzle to myself, asking my soul again and again 'Why are you downcast? Why do you distress me?' But my soul had no answer to give. If I had said 'Wait for God's help', she did not obey. And in this she was right because, to her, the well-loved man whom she had lost was better and more real than the shadowy being in whom I would have her trust.

St Augustine, *Confessions* IV.4

Faith

O Friend! I know not which way I must look
For comfort, being as I am, opprest,
To think that now our life is only drest
For show; mean handy-work of craftsman, cook,
Or groom! – We must run glittering like a brook
In the open sunshine, or we are unblest:
The wealthiest man among us is the best:
No grandeur now in nature or in book
Delights us – Rapine, avarice, expense,
This is idolatry; and these we adore;
Plain living and high thinking are no more:
The homely beauty of the good old cause
Is gone; our peace, our fearful innocence,
And pure religion breathing household laws.

William Wordsworth

Nevertheless, when the Son of man comes, will he find faith on earth?

The Gospel according to St Luke 18.8

. . . and, bold with joy,
Forth from his dark and lonely hiding-place,
(Portentous sight!) the owlet Atheism,
Sailing on obscene wings athwart the noon,
Drops his blue-fringéd lids, and holds them close,
And hooting at the glorious sun in Heaven,
Cries out, 'Where is it?'

Samuel Taylor Coleridge, 'Fears in solitude', ll. 80–6

. . . In short, no one would allow that he could not see these much-admired clothes; because, in doing so, he would have declared himself either a simpleton or unfit for his office. Certainly, none of the

Emperor's various suits had ever made so great an impression as these invisible ones.

'But the Emperor has nothing at all on!' said a little child. 'Listen to the voice of innocence!' exclaimed his father, and what the child had said was whispered one to another.

'But he has nothing at all on!' at last cried out all the people.

Hans Christian Andersen, *Fairy Tales*, 'The Emperor's New Clothes'

l. 182   Just when we are safest, there's a sunset-touch,
      A fancy from a flower-bell, someone's death,
      A chorus-ending from Euripides, –
      And that's enough for fifty hopes and fears
      As old and new at once as nature's self,

      To rap and knock and enter in our soul,
      Take hands and dance there, a fantastic ring,
      Round the ancient idol, on his base again, –
      The grand Perhaps! We look on helplessly.
      There the old misgivings, crooked questions are –
      This good God, – what he could do, if he would,
      Would, if he could – then must have done long since:
      If so, when, where and how? some way must be, –
      Once feel about, and soon or late you hit
      Some sense, in which it might be after all.
      Why not, 'The Way, the Truth, the Life?'

l. 209   All we have gained then by our unbelief
      Is a life of doubt diversified by faith,
      For one of faith diversified by doubt:
      We called the chess-board white, – we call it black.

l. 626   'What think ye of Christ', friend? when all's done and said
      Like you this Christianity or not?
      It may be false, but will you wish it true?
      Has it your vote to be so if it can?

Faith

l. 647 Pure faith indeed – you know not what you ask!
        Naked belief in God the Omnipotent,
        Omniscient, Omnipresent, sears too much
        The sense of conscious creatures to be borne,
        It were the seeing him, no flesh shall dare.

l. 693 No, when the fight begins within himself,
        A man's worth something. God stoops o'er his head,
        Satan looks up between his feet – both tug –
        He's left, himself, i'the middle: the soul wakes
        And grows. Prolong that battle through his life!
        Never leave growing till the life to come!

l. 724 The sum of all is – yes, my doubt is great,
        My faith's still greater, then my faith's enough.

Robert Browning, 'Bishop Blougram's Apology'

Ich habe Gott gesucht und fand ihm nicht
Ich schrie empor und bettelte ins Licht.
Da, wie ich weinend bin zurückgegangen,
Faßt's leise meine Schulter: 'Ich bin hier,
Ich habe dich gesucht und bin bei dir'.
Und Gott ist mit mir heimgegangen.

I searched for God and did not find Him,
I cried heavenwards and begged my way into the light.
Then, as I came back weeping,
Someone gently grasped my shoulder: 'I am here,
I have searched for thee and am beside thee'.
And God came home with me.

Gustav Schüler, 'Der Gottsucher'

'I think I'll go and meet her', said Alice, for, though the flowers were interesting enough, she felt that it would be far grander to have a talk with a real Queen.

'You can't possibly do that', said the Rose: '*I* should advise you to walk the other way'.

This sounded nonsense to Alice, so she said nothing, but set off at once towards the Red Queen. To her surprise she lost sight of her in a moment, and found herself walking in at the front door again.

A little provoked, she drew back, and, after looking everywhere for the Queen (whom she spied out at last, a long way off), she thought she would try the plan, this time, of walking in the opposite direction.

It succeeded beautifully. She had not been walking a minute before she found herself face to face with the Red Queen, and full in sight of the hill she had been so long aiming at.

Lewis Carroll, *Through the Looking Glass*, Chapter 2

Say not the struggle nought availeth,
The labour and the wounds are vain,
The enemy faints not, nor faileth,
And as things have been they remain.

If hopes were dupes, fears may be liars;
It may be, in yon smoke conceal'd,
Your comrades chase e'en now the fliers,
And, but for you, possess the field.

For while the tired waves, vainly breaking,
Seem here no painful inch to gain,
Far back, through creeks and inlets making,
Comes silent, flooding in, the main.

And not by eastern windows only,
When daylight comes, comes in the light;

Faith

In front the sun climbs slow, how slowly!
But westward, look, the land is bright!

Arthur Hugh Clough

If Catholics and Protestants both try, while bearing each other in mind, to get closer and closer to their own standards, then (since the standard is the same for both), they and their basic demands must begin more and more to coincide with each other.

Hans Küng, *The Council and Reunion*, p. 84

Thus says the LORD of hosts: In those days ten men from the nations of every tongue shall take hold of the robe of a Jew, saying, 'Let us go with you, for we have heard that God is with you.'

Zechariah 8.23

Walk about Sion, and go round about her: and tell the towers thereof.
Mark well her bulwarks, set up her houses: that ye may tell them that come after.

Psalm 48.11–12

I look abroad upon Nature, I think of the best part of our species, I lean upon my friends, and I meditate upon the Scriptures, especially the Gospel of St John, and my creed rises up of itself with the ease of an exhalation yet a fabric of adamant.

William Wordsworth, Letter to Sir George Beaumont, 28 May 1825

If any man will do his will, he shall know of the doctrine, whether it be of God.

The Gospel according to St John 7.17 (King James Version)

I should now like to ask how important it is deemed to be that the philosopher's experience should fall into the form of an inward colloquy, with one part of his thought addressing another as though with the voice of God. I have a special and personal interest in challenging the colloquy form, because of an obstacle I remember encountering in my own adolescence. I had myself (at least this is the impression I retain) been reared in a personalism which might satisfy the most ardent of Dr Buber's disciples. I thought of myself as set over against deity as one man faces another across a table, except that God was invisible and indefinitely great. And I hoped that he would signify his presence by way of colloquy; but neither out of the scripture I read nor in the prayers I tried to make did any mental voice address me. I believe at that time anything would have satisfied me, but nothing came: no 'other' stood beside me, no shadow of presence fell upon me. I owe my liberation from this *impasse*, as far as I can remember, to reading Spinoza's Ethics. Those phrases which now strike me as so flat and sinister, so ultimately atheistic, *Deus sive Natura* (God, or call it Nature), *Deus, quatenus consideratur ut constituens essentiam humanae mentis* (God, in so far as he is regarded as constituting the being of the human mind) – these phrases were to me light and liberation, not because I was or desired to be a pantheist, but because I could not find the wished-for colloquy with God.

Undoubtedly I misunderstood Spinoza, in somewhat the same fashion as (to quote a high example) St Augustine misunderstood Plotinus, turning him to Christian uses. Here, anyhow, is what I took from Spinozism. I would no longer attempt, with the Psalmist, 'to set God before my face'. I would see him as the underlying cause of my thinking, especially of those thoughts in which I tried to think of him. I would dare to hope that sometimes my thought would become diaphanous, so that there should be some perception of the divine cause shining through the created effect, as a deep pool, settling into a clear tranquillity, permits us to see the spring in the bottom of it from which its waters rise. I would dare to hope that through a second cause the First Cause might be felt, when the second cause in question was itself a spirit, made in the image of the divine Spirit, and perpetually welling up out of his creative act.

Such things, I say, I dared to hope for, and I will not say that my hope was in any way remarkably fulfilled, but I will say that by so viewing my attempted work of prayer, I was rid of the frustration which had baffled me before. And this is why, when Germans set their eyeballs and pronounce the terrific words 'He speaks to thee' (Er redet dich an) I am sure, indeed, that they are saying something, but I am still more sure that they are not speaking to my condition.

Austin Farrer, *The Glass of Vision*, pp. 7–8

The Pauline letters are letters from St Paul to the churches, not letters from God to St Paul.

James Barr, *The Bible in the Modern World*, p. 123

Behold, if thou canst, thou soul heavily burdened by the body of corruption, laden with earthly conceits many and diverse, behold if thou canst: God is Truth. It is written, 'For God is light' – not the light seen by these eyes of ours, but that which the heart sees upon hearing of the words 'He is Truth'. Ask not, what is Truth? At once will rise the fogs of material images, the thick chords of phantasm, and darken that clear empyrean which shone forth for a single instant upon your sight at that word, 'Truth'. In that instant, that flash of vision that touches you with the word 'Truth', hold fast – if you can.

St Augustine, *The Trinity*, VIII.2.3

Batter my heart, three-personed God, for you
As yet but knock, breathe, shine, and seek to mend;
That I may rise and stand, o'erthrow me and bend
Your force to break, blow, burn and make me new.

I, like an usurped town to another due,
Labour to admit you, but O, to no end.
Reason, your viceroy in me, me should defend,
But is captived and proves weak or untrue.
Yet dearly I love you and would be loved fain,
But am betrothed unto your enemy.
Divorce me, untie, or break that knot again,
Take me to you, imprison me, for I,
Except you enthrall me, never shall be free,
Nor ever chaste, unless you ravish me.

John Donne

And Jacob was left alone; and a man wrestled with him until the breaking of the day. When the man saw that he did not prevail against Jacob, he touched the hollow of his thigh; and Jacob's thigh was put out of joint as he wrestled with him. Then he said, 'Let me go, for the day is breaking.' But Jacob said, 'I will not let you go, unless you bless me.' And he said to him, 'What is your name?' And he said, 'Jacob.' Then he said, 'Your name shall no more be called Jacob, but Israel, for you have striven with God and with men, and have prevailed.' Then Jacob asked him, 'Tell me, I pray, your name.' But he said, 'Why is it that you ask my name?' And there he blessed him. So Jacob called the name of the place Peniel, saying, 'For I have seen God face to face, and yet my life is preserved.' The sun rose upon him as he passed Peniel, limping because of his thigh.

Genesis 32.24–31

Come, O thou Traveller unknown,
Whom still I hold, but cannot see,
My company before is gone,
And I am left alone with Thee

With Thee all night I mean to stay,
And wrestle till the break of day . . .

Yield to me now, for I am weak,
But confident in self-despair,
Speak to my heart, in blessings speak,
Be conquer'd by my instant prayer!
Speak, or Thou never hence shalt move,
And tell me if thy Name is Love?

Charles Wesley, 'Wrestling Jacob'

The very God! Think, Abib; dost thou think!
So, the all-great, were the all-loving too –
So, through the thunder comes a human voice
Saying, 'O heart I made, a heart beats here!
Face, my hands fashioned, see it in myself!
Thou hast no power nor mayest conceive of mine,
But love I gave thee, with myself to love,
And thou must love me who have died for thee!'
The madman saith He said so: it is strange.

Robert Browning, 'An Epistle containing the strange medical experience of
Karshish the Arab physician', ll. 304–9

A painter of the Umbrian school
Designed upon a gesso ground
The nimbus of the Baptized God.
The wilderness is cracked and browned
But through the water pale and thin
Still shine the unoffending feet
And there above the painter set
The Father and the Paraclete.

T. S. Eliot, 'Mr Eliot's Sunday Morning Service'

Profitable Wonders

In the life of Moses, in Hebrew folklore, there is a remarkable passage. Moses finds a shepherd in the desert. He spends the day with the shepherd and helps him milk his ewes, and at the end of the day he sees that the shepherd puts the best milk he has in a wooden bowl, which he places on a flat stone some distance away. So Moses asks him what it is for, and the shepherd replies, 'This is God's milk'. Moses is puzzled and asks him what he means. The shepherd says, 'I always take the best milk I possess, and I bring it as an offering to God'. Moses, who is far more sophisticated than the shepherd with his naive faith, asks, 'And does God drink it?' 'Yes', replies the shepherd, 'He does'. Then Moses feels compelled to enlighten the poor shepherd and he explains that God, being pure Spirit, does not drink milk. Yet the shepherd is sure that He does, and so they have a short argument, which ends with Moses telling the shepherd to hide behind the bushes to find out whether in fact God does come to drink the milk.

Moses then goes out to pray in the desert. The shepherd hides, the night comes, and in the moonlight the shepherd sees a little fox that comes trotting from the desert, looks right, looks left and heads straight towards the milk, which he laps up, and disappears into the desert again. The next morning Moses finds the shepherd quite depressed and downcast. 'What's the matter?' he asks. The shepherd says, 'You were right, God is pure spirit and He doesn't want my milk'. Moses is surprised. He says, 'You should be happy. You know more about God than you did before'. 'Yes I do', says the shepherd, 'but the only thing I could do to express my love for Him has been taken away from me'. Moses sees the point. He retires into the desert and prays hard. In the night in a vision, God speaks to him and says, 'Moses, you were wrong. It is true that I am pure spirit. Nevertheless I always accepted with gratitude the milk which the shepherd offered me, as the expression of his love, but since, being pure spirit, I do not need the milk, I shared it with the little fox, who is very fond of milk'.

Anthony Bloom, *School for Prayer*, p. 22

Faith

Scripture knows no 'Omnipresence', neither the expression nor the meaning it expresses; it knows only the God who is where he wills to be, and is not where he wills not to be, the *deus mobilis*, who is no mere universally extended being, but an august mystery, that comes and goes, approaches and withdraws, has its time and its hour, and may be far and near in infinite degrees, 'closer than breathing' to us or miles remote from us.

Rudolf Otto, *The Idea of the Holy*, Appendix VIII

Sero te amavi, pulchritudo tam antiqua et tam nova, sero te amavi! et ecce intus eras et ego foris, et ibi te quaerebam.

Late have I loved you, beauty so old and so new: late have I loved you. And see, you were within and I was in the external world and sought you there . . .

St Augustine, *Confessions*, X.27, tr. H. Chadwick

Keep me, O Lord, while I tarry on this earth, in a daily serious seeking after thee and in a believing affectionate walking with thee; that when thou comest, I may be found not hiding my talent, nor left asleep with my lamp unfurnished; but waiting and longing for my Lord, my glorious God, for ever and ever.

Richard Baxter

So too let him rejoice and delight at finding you who are beyond discovery rather than fail to find you by supposing you to be discoverable.

St Augustine, *Confessions*, I.6, tr. H. Chadwick

Stand in awe, and sin not: commune with your own heart, and in
    your chamber, and be still.
Offer the sacrifice of righteousness: and put thou thy trust in the
    Lord.
There be many that say: who shall show us any good?
Lord, lift thou up: the light of thy countenance upon us.
Thou hast put gladness in my heart: since the time that their
    corn, and wine, and oil, increased.
I will lay me down in peace, and take my rest: for it is thou, Lord,
    only that makest me dwell in safety.

Psalm 4.4–9

A senior devil's advice to a young tempter:
. . . if ever he consciously directs his prayers 'Not to what I think thou
art but to what thou knowest thyself to be', our situation is, for the
moment, desperate.

C. S. Lewis, *The Screwtape Letters*, 4

And Moses said, 'I will turn aside and see this great sight, why the
bush is not burnt.' When the LORD saw that he turned aside to see,
God called to him out of the bush, 'Moses, Moses.' And he said,
'Here am I.' Then he said, 'Do not come near: put off your shoes
from your feet, for the place on which you are standing is holy
ground.' And he said, 'I am the God of your father, the God of
Abraham, the God of Isaac, and the God of Jacob.' And Moses hid
his face; for he was afraid to look at God.

Exodus 3.3–6

In all this I was much moved with love for my fellow Christians,
wishing that they might see and know what I was seeing; I wanted it
to comfort them, for the vision was shown for everyone.

[16]

I am not good because of the showing unless I love God better; and if you love God better, it is meant more for you than for me. I am not saying this to the wise, for they know it well; but I am saying it to those of you who are ignorant, to support and comfort you: we all need support. Indeed I was not shown that God loved me better than the lowest soul that is in a state of grace, for I am sure that there are many who never had a showing or vision, but only the normal teaching of Holy Church, and who love God better than I do. For if I look solely at myself, I am really nothing; but as one of mankind in general, I am, I hope, in oneness of love with all my fellow Christians; for upon this oneness depends the life of all who shall be saved.

Julian of Norwich, Revelations of Divine Love, Chapters 8 and 9

In the year that King Uzziah died I saw the Lord sitting upon a throne, high and lifted up; and his train filled the temple. Above him stood the seraphim: each had six wings; with two he covered his face, and with two he covered his feet, and with two he flew. And one called to another and said:

'Holy, holy, holy, is the LORD of hosts;
the whole earth is full of his glory.'

And the foundations of the thresholds shook at the voice of him who called, and the house was filled with smoke. And I said: 'Woe is me! For I am lost; for I am a man of unclean lips, and I dwell in the midst of a people of unclean lips; for mine eyes have seen the King, the LORD of hosts!'

Then flew one of the seraphim to me, having in his hand a live coal which he had taken with tongs from the altar. And he touched my mouth, and said: 'Behold, this has touched your lips; your iniquity is taken away, and your sin forgiven.' And I heard the voice of the LORD saying, 'Whom shall I send, and who will go for us?' And I said, 'Here am I; send me.'

Isaiah 6.1–8

'What to me is the multitude of your sacrifices?' says the LORD: 'I have had enough of burnt offerings of rams and the fat of fed beasts; I do not delight in the blood of bulls, or of lambs, or of he-goats. When you come to appear before me, who requires of you this trampling of my courts? Bring no more vain offerings; incense is an abomination to me. New moon and sabbath and the calling of assemblies – I cannot endure iniquity and solemn assembly. Your new moons and your appointed feasts my soul hates; they have become a burden to me; I am weary of bearing them. When you spread forth your hands, I will hide my eyes from you; even though you make many prayers, I will not listen; your hands are full of blood. Wash yourselves; make yourselves clean; remove the evil of your doings from before my eyes; cease to do evil, learn to do good; seek justice, correct oppression; defend the fatherless, plead for the widow.'

'Come now, let us reason together,' says the LORD: 'though your sins are like scarlet, they shall be as white as snow; though they are red like crimson, they shall become like wool.'

Isaiah 1.11–18

. . . for he who does not love his brother whom he has seen, cannot love God whom he has not seen.

The First Epistle of St John 4.20

'God is love'. What outward appearance, what form, what stature, hands or feet, has love? None can say; and yet love has feet, which take us to the Church, love has hands which give to the poor, love has eyes which give intelligence of him who is in need – as the Psalm says: 'Blessed is he who bethinks him of the needy and poor.' Love has ears, of which the Lord says: 'He that has ears for hearing, let him hear.' All these are not members set each in their own place: he that has charity sees the whole at once with the understanding's

[18]

grasp. Dwell there and you shall be dwelt in: abide, and there shall be abiding in you. My brothers, one does not love what one cannot see. Why then, when you hear the praise of charity, are you stirred to acclamation and applause? What have I displayed to your eyes? No vivid colours, no gold or silver, no gems of the treasure-house. My own face has not changed in speaking: this body of mine looks as it did when I entered the church, and so do all of you. You hear the praise of charity, and your voices ring out. Certainly there is nothing for you to see. But let that same delight in charity which makes you acclaim it, lead you to hold it fast in your heart. Listen to me, my brothers: here is a great treasure, which I would urge you with all the power that God gives me to win for yourselves.

St Augustine, *Homilies on 1 John*, 7.10

Lucia
Vergine di Siracusa
Martire di Cristo
In questo tempio
Riposa
All'Italia al mondo
Implori
Luce Pace

Lucy
Virgin of Syracuse
Martyr of Christ
in this temple
rests
To Italy to the world
she would implore
Light Peace

Santa Lucia's Epitaph, from the Church of S. Geremia in Venice

For this reason I bow my knees before the Father, from whom every family in heaven and on earth is named, that according to the riches of his glory he may grant you to be strengthened with might through his Spirit in the inner man; and that Christ may dwell in your hearts through faith; that you, being rooted and grounded in love, may have power to comprehend with all the saints what is the breadth and length and height and depth, and to know the love of Christ, which surpasses knowledge, that you may be filled with all the fulness of God.

Now to him who by the power at work within us is able to do far more abundantly than all that we ask or think, to him be glory in the church and in Christ Jesus to all generations, for ever and ever. Amen.

St Paul's Epistle to the Ephesians 3.14–20

O taste, and see, how gracious the Lord is.

Psalm 34.8

Creation: the work of God; and of people made in God's image

The God whom faith tries to find is first of all God the Father Almighty, Maker of heaven and earth. To begin here is a good corrective to the moralistic notion that Christian faith is all about duty. The God revealed in the Bible is an artist as well as a legislator. God wants, shapes and enjoys as well as commanding and judging. To say, 'Do look! Do pay attention to this!' is as Christian as to say, 'Obey!'

The glory of nature is a picture of God's sometimes terrifying magnificence. To praise God's work is a kind of worship, not proving but celebrating the majesty of the Creator.

Human beings, made in God's image, are characteristically makers, godlike in exuberant creation. Their works, like God's, go beyond what might seem to be needed. Divine creation is supposed to be quite different from human making because it is 'from nothing'; but the difference is not the whole story. Human creation, in its way, brings into existence something new, more than its bare ingredients. To show one another works of creation, human and divine, is a way of glorifying God.

Praise the Lord, O my soul: O Lord my God, thou art become
   exceeding glorious; thou art clothed with majesty and honour.
Thou deckest thyself with light as it were with a garment: and
   spreadest out the heavens like a curtain.

Who layeth the beams of his chambers in the waters: and
    maketh the clouds his chariot, and walketh upon the wings of
    the wind.
He maketh his angels spirits: and his ministers a flaming fire.
He laid the foundations of the earth: that it never should move at
    any time.
Thou coveredst it with the deep like as with a garment: the
    waters stand in the hills.
At thy rebuke they flee: at the voice of thy thunder they are
    afraid.
They go up as high as the hills, and down to the valleys beneath:
    even unto the place which thou hast appointed for them.
Thou hast set them their bounds which they shall not pass:
    neither turn again to cover the earth.
He sendeth the springs into the rivers: which run among the
    hills.
All beasts of the field drink thereof: and the wild asses quench
    their thirst.
Beside them shall the fowls of the air have their habitation: and
    sing among the branches.
He watereth the hills from above: the earth is filled with the fruit
    of thy works.
He bringeth forth grass for the cattle: and green herb for the
    service of man.
That he may bring food out of the earth, and wine that maketh
    glad the heart of man: and oil to make him a cheerful counten-
    ance, and bread to strengthen man's heart.
The trees of the Lord also are full of sap: even the cedars of
    Libanus which he hath planted.
Wherein the birds make their nests: and the fir-trees are a
    dwelling for the stork.
The high hills are a refuge for the wild goats: and so are the stony
    rocks for the coneys.

He appointeth the moon for certain seasons: and the sun
knoweth his going down.

Thou makest darkness that it may be night: wherein all the
beasts of the forest do move.

The lions roaring after their prey: do seek their meat from God.

The sun ariseth, and they get them away together: and lay them
down in their dens.

Man goeth forth to his work, and to his labour: until the evening.

O Lord, how manifold are thy works: in wisdom hast thou made
them all; the earth is full of thy riches.

So is the great and wide sea also: wherein are things creeping
innumerable, both small and great beasts.

There go the ships, and there is that Leviathan, whom thou hast
made to take his pastime therein.

These wait all upon thee: that thou mayest give them meat in
due season.

When thou givest it them they gather it: and when thou openest
thy hand they are filled with good.

When thou hidest thy face they are troubled: when thou takest
away their breath they die, and are turned again to their dust.

When thou lettest thy breath go forth they shall be made: and
thou shalt renew the face of the earth.

The glorious Majesty of the Lord shall endure for ever: the Lord
shall rejoice in his works.

The earth shall tremble at the look of him: if he do but touch the
hills, they shall smoke.

I will sing unto the Lord as long as I live: I will praise my God
while I have my being.

And so shall my words please him: my joy shall be in the Lord.

As for sinners, they shall be consumed out of the earth, and the
ungodly shall come to an end: praise thou the Lord, O my
soul, praise the Lord.

Psalm 104

Suppose, my brethren, a man should make for his betrothed a ring, and she should prefer the ring given her to the betrothed who made it for her, would not her heart be convicted of infidelity in respect of the very gift of her betrothed, though what she loved were what he gave. Certainly let her love his gift; but if she should say, 'The ring is enough, I do not want to see his face again', what should we say of her? . . . Yet surely the pledge is given by the betrothed, just that in his pledge he himself may be loved. Even so, God has given you all these things: therefore, love him who gave them. There is more that he would give you, even himself, their Maker.

St Augustine, Homilies on 1 John, II

In this vision he also showed a little thing, the size of a hazel-nut in the palm of my hand, and it was as round as a ball. I looked at it with my mind's eye and thought, 'What can this be?' And the answer came to me, 'It is all that is made.' I wondered how it could last, for it was so small I thought it might suddenly have disappeared. And the answer in my mind was, 'It lasts and will last for ever because God loves it; and everything exists in the same way by the love of God.'

Julian of Norwich, Revelations of Divine Love, Chapter 5

In his hand are all the corners of the earth: and the strength of
    the hills is his also.
The sea is his, and he made it: and his hands prepared the dry
    land.

Psalm 95.4–5 (Venite)

And what is this God? I asked the earth, and it answered 'I am not he'; and everything in the earth made the same confession. I asked

[24]

the sea and the deeps and the creeping things, and they replied, 'We are not your God; seek above us'. I asked the fleeting winds, and the whole air with its inhabitants answered, 'Anaximenes was deceived; I am not God'. I asked the heavens, the sun, moon and stars, and they answered, 'Neither are we the God whom you seek'. And I replied to all these things which stand around the door of my flesh: 'You have told me about my God, that you are not he. Tell me something about him'. And with a loud voice they all cried out, 'He made us'. My question had come from my observation of them, and their reply came from their beauty of order. And I turned my thoughts into myself and said, 'Who are you?' And I answered, 'A man'. For see, there is in me both a body and a soul; the one without, the other within. In which of these should I have sought my God, whom I had already sought with my body from earth to heaven, as far as I was able to send those messengers – the beams of my eyes? But the inner part is the better part; for to it, as both ruler and judge, all messengers of the senses report the answers of both heaven and earth and all the things therein, who said, 'We are not God, but he made us'. My inner man knew these things through the ministry of the outer man, and I, the inner man, knew all this, I, the soul, through the senses of my body. I asked the whole frame of earth about my God, and it answered, 'I am not he, but he made me'.

St Augustine, *Confessions*, X.6

The spacious firmament on high
With all the blue ethereal sky,
And spangled heavens, a shining frame,
Their great Original proclaim:
The unwearied sun, from day to day,
Does his Creator's power display,
And publishes to every land
The work of an almighty hand.

Soon as the evening shades prevail,
The moon takes up the wondrous tale,
And nightly to the listening earth
Repeats the story of her birth:
While all the stars that round her burn,
And all the planets in their turn,
Confirm the tidings as they roll,
And spread the truth from pole to pole.

What though in solemn silence all
Move round the dark terrestrial ball?
What though no real voice nor sound
Amid their radiant orbs be found?
In reason's ear they all rejoice,
And utter forth a glorious voice,
For ever singing as they shine,
'The hand that made us is divine.'

Joseph Addison

Thou dost preserve the stars from wrong;
And the most ancient heavens, through Thee, are fresh and
strong.

William Wordsworth, 'Ode to Duty'

Thou, silent form, dost tease us out of thought
As doth Eternity.

John Keats, 'Ode on a Grecian Urn'

On what grounds do you call millions of light-years of inter-galactic
space a 'waste'? A waste of what? Of space?

John Austin Baker, *The Foolishness of God*, p. 52

Then the Lord answered Job out of the whirlwind, and said,

Who is this that darkeneth counsel by words without knowledge?

Gird up now thy loins like a man; for I will demand of thee, and
answer thou me.

Where wast thou when I laid the foundations of the earth? declare,
if thou hast understanding.

Who hath laid the measures thereof, if thou knowest? or who hast
stretched the line upon it?

Whereupon are the foundations thereof fastened? or who laid the
corner stone thereof?

When the morning stars sang together, and all the sons of God
shouted for joy?

Or who shut up the sea with doors, when it brake forth, as if it had
issued out of the womb?

When I made the cloud the garment thereof, and thick darkness a
swaddlingband for it,

And brake up for it my decreed place, and set bars and doors,

And said, Hitherto shalt thou come, but no further, and here shall
thy proud waves be stayed?

Hast thou commanded the morning since thy days; and caused the
dayspring to know his place;

That it might take hold of the ends of the earth, that the wicked
might be shaken out of it?

It is turned as clay to the seal; and they stand as a garment.

And from the wicked their light is withholden, and the high arm
shall be broken.

Hast thou entered into the springs of the sea? Or hast thou walked
in the search of the depth?

Have the gates of death been opened unto thee? or hast thou seen
the doors of the shadow of death?

Hast thou perceived the breadth of the earth? declare thou if thou
knowest it all.

Where is the way where light dwelleth? and as for darkness, where
is the place thereof,

That thou shouldest take it to the bound thereof, and that thou
shouldest know the paths to the house thereof?

Knowest thou it, because thou wast then born? or because the
number of thy days is great?

Hast thou entered into the treasures of the snow? or hast thou seen
the treasures of the hail?

Which I have reserved against the time of trouble, against the day
of battle and war?

By what way is the light parted, which scattereth the east wind
upon the earth?

Who hath divided a watercourse for the overflowing of waters, or a
way for the lightning of thunder;

To cause it to rain on the earth, where no man is; on the
wilderness, wherein there is no man;

To satisfy the desolate and waste ground; and to cause the bud of
the tender herb to spring forth?

Hath the rain a father, or who hath begotten the drops of dew?

Out of whose womb came the ice? and the hoary frost of heaven,
who hath gendered it?

The waters are hid as with a stone, and the face of the deep is frozen.

Canst thou bind the sweet influences of Pleiades, or loose the
bands of Orion?

Canst thou bring forth Mazzaroth in his season? or canst thou
guide Arcturus with his sons?

Knowest thou the ordinances of heaven? Canst thou get the
dominion thereof in the earth?

Canst thou lift up thy voice to the clouds, that abundance of waters
may cover thee?

Canst thou send lightnings, that they may go, and say unto thee,
Here we are?

Who hath put wisdom in the inward parts? or who hath given
understanding to the heart?

Who can number the clouds in wisdom? or who can stay the bottles
of heaven,

Creation

When the dust groweth into hardness, and the clods cleave fast
    together?
Wilt thou hunt the prey for the lion? or fill the appetite of the young
    lions,
When they crouch in their dens, and abide in the covert to lie in
    wait?
Who provideth for the raven his food? When his young ones cry
    unto God, they wander for lack of meat.

Job 38 (King James Version)

Postern of Fate, the Desert Gate, Disaster's Cavern, Fort of Fear,
The Portal of Bagdad am I, the Doorway of Diarbekir.

The Persian Dawn with new desires may net the flushing
    mountain spires:
But my gaunt buttress still rejects the suppliance of those
    mellow fires.

Pass not beneath, O Caravan, or pass not singing. Have you
    heard
That silence where the birds are dead yet something singeth like
    a bird?

Pass not beneath! Men say there blows in stony deserts still a
    rose
But with no scarlet to her leaf – and from whose heart no
    perfume flows.

Wilt thou bloom red where she buds pale, thy sister rose? Wilt
    thou not fail
When noonday flashes like a flail? Leave nightingale the caravan!

Pass then, pass all! 'Bagdad!' ye cry, and down the billows of blue
    sky
Ye beat the bell that beats to hell, and who shall thrust ye back?
    Not I.

The Sun who flashes through the head and paints the shadows
    green and red, –
The Sun shall eat thy fleshless dead, O Caravan, O Caravan!

And one who licks his lips for thirst with fevered eyes shall face
    in fear
The palms that wave, the streams that burst, his last mirage, O
    Caravan!

And one – the bird-voiced singing man – shall fall behind thee,
    Caravan!
And God shall meet him in the night, and he shall sing as best
    he can.

And one the Bedouin shall slay, and one sand-stricken on the
    way
Go dark and blind; and one shall say – 'How lonely is the
    Caravan!'

Pass out beneath, O Caravan, Doom's Caravan, Death's Caravan!
I had not told ye, fools, so much, save that I heard your singing-
    man.

                       James Elroy Flecker, 'The Gates of Damascus'

Oberon: That very time I saw, but thou couldst not,
            Flying between the cold moon and the earth,
            Cupid all arm'd: a certain aim he took
            At a fair vestal throned by the west,

And loos'd his love-shaft smartly from his bow,
As it should pierce a hundred thousand hearts;
But I might see young Cupid's fiery shaft
Quench'd in the chaste beams of the watery moon,
And the imperial votaress passed on,
In maiden-meditation, fancy-free.
Yet marked I where the bolt of Cupid fell:
It fell upon a little wayside flower,
Before milk-white, now purple with love's wound,
And maidens call it, Love-in-idleness.

William Shakespeare, *A Midsummer Night's Dream*, II.1

. . . No stir of air was there,
Not so much life as on a summer's day
Robs not one light seed from the feathered grass,
But where the dead leaf fell, there did it rest.

John Keats, 'Hyperion', I.7

. . . a brown fog covered the ground, and a small, tomato-red sun, like a jellyfish floating in the sky, appeared and disappeared as the air grew thicker or finer.

Edwin Muir, *An Autobiography*, p. 96

Othello: Keep up your bright swords, for the dew will rust them.

William Shakespeare, *Othello*, I.1

. . . the moon lifting her silver rim
Above a cloud, and with a gradual swim
Coming into the blue with all her light.

John Keats, 'I stood tip-toe upon a little hill', ll. 113–15

. . . and let the stars
Come forth, perhaps without one quiet thought.

William Wordsworth, *The Prelude*, III, ll. 257–8

Zwei Dinge erfüllen das Gemüth mit immer neuer und zu-
nehmender Bewunderung und Ehrfurcht, je öfter und anhaltender
sich das Nachdenken damit beschäftigt: der bestirnte Himmel über
mir, und das moralische Gesetz in mir.

Two things fill the mind with ever new and increasing wonder and
awe, the more often and intensely reflection is occupied with them:
the starry heaven above me and the moral law within me.

Immanuel Kant, *Critique of Practical Reason*, Conclusion

The world is too much with us; late and soon,
Getting and spending, we lay waste our powers:
Little we see in Nature that is ours;
We have given our hearts away, a sordid boon!
This Sea that bares her bosom to the moon;
The winds that will be howling at all hours,
And are up-gathered now like sleeping flowers;
For this, for everything, we are out of tune;
It moves us not. – Great God! I'd rather be
A Pagan suckled in a creed outworn;
So might I, standing on this pleasant lea,
Have glimpses that would make me less forlorn;
Have sight of Proteus rising from the sea;
Or hear old Triton blow his wreathèd horn.

William Wordsworth

Too wearily had we and song
Been left to look and left to long,
Yea song and we to long and look,
Since thine acquainted feet forsook
The mountain where the Muses hymn
For Sinai and the Seraphim.
Now in both the mountains shine
Dress thy countenance, twice divine!
From Moses and the Muses draw
The Tables of thy double law!
His red-born fount, and Castaly
Let the one rock bring forth to thee
Renewing so from either spring
The songs which both thy countries sing.
For we shall fear, lest, heaven'd thus long,
Thou shalt forget thy native song
And mar thy mortal melodies
With broken stammer of the skies.
Ah! let the sweet birds of the Lord
With earth's music make accord;
Teach how the Crucifix may be
Carven from the laurel tree,
Fruit of the Hesperides
Burnish take on Eden-trees,
The Muses' sacred grove be wet
With the red dew of Olivet.

Francis Thompson, 'To a poet, breaking silence'

But will God indeed dwell on the earth? Behold, heaven and the heaven of heavens cannot contain thee; how much less this house that I have built? Yet have regard to the prayer of thy servant, and to his supplication, O LORD my God, hearkening to the cry and to the

prayer which thy servant prays before thee this day; that thy eyes may
be open night and day toward this house, the place of which thou
hast said, 'My name shall be there', that thou mayest hearken to the
prayer which thy servant offers toward this place. And hearken thou
to the supplication of thy servant and of thy people Israel, when they
pray toward this place; yea, hear thou in heaven thy dwelling place;
and when thou hearest, forgive.

1 Kings 8.27–30

The Lord, even the most mighty God, hath spoken: and hath called
   the world, from the rising up of the sun, unto the going down
   thereof.
Out of Sion hath God appeared: in perfect beauty.
Our God shall come, and shall not keep silence: there shall go
   before him a consuming fire, and a mighty tempest shall be
   stirred up round about him.
He shall call the heaven from above: and the earth, that he may
   judge his people.
Gather my saints together unto me: those that have made a
   covenant with me with sacrifice.
And the heaven shall declare his righteousness: for God is Judge
   himself.
Hear, O my people, for I will speak: I myself will testify against
   thee, O Israel; for I am God, even thy God.
I will not reprove thee because of thy sacrifices, or for thy burnt-
   offerings: because they were not alway before me.
I will take no bullock out of thine house: nor he-goat out of thy
   folds.
For all the beasts of the forest are mine: and so are the cattle upon a
   thousand hills.
I know all the fowls upon the mountains: and the wild beasts of the
   field are in my sight.

If I be hungry, I will not tell thee: for the whole world is mine, and all that is therein.

Thinkest thou that I will eat bull's flesh: and drink the blood of goats?

Offer unto God thanksgiving: and pay thy vows unto the most Highest.

And call upon me in the time of trouble: so will I hear thee, and thou shalt praise me.

But unto the ungodly said God: Why dost thou preach my laws, and takest my covenant in thy mouth;

Whereas thou hatest to be reformed: and hast cast my words behind thee?

When thou sawest a thief, thou consentedst unto him: and hast been partaker with the adulterers.

Thou hast let thy mouth speak wickedness: and with thy tongue thou hast set forth deceit.

Thou satest, and spakest against thy brother: yea, and hast slandered thine own mother's son.

These things hast thou done, and I held my tongue, and thou thoughtest wickedly, that I am even such a one as thyself: but I will reprove thee, and set before thee the things that thou hast done.

O consider this, ye that forget God: lest I pluck you away, and there be none to deliver you.

Whoso offereth me thanks and praise, he honoureth me: and to him that ordereth his conversation right will I show the salvation of God.

Psalm 50

Tyger! Tyger! burning bright
In the forests of the night,
What immortal hand or eye
Could frame thy fearful symmetry?

Profitable Wonders

In what distant deeps or skies
Burnt the fire of thine eyes?
On what wings dare he aspire?
What the hand dare seize the fire?

And what shoulder, and what art,
Could twist the sinews of thy heart?
And when the heart began to beat,
What dread hand? and what dread feet?

What the hammer? What the chain?
In what furnace was thy brain?
What the anvil? What dread grasp
Dare its deadly terrors clasp?

When the stars threw down their spears,
And watered heaven with their tears,
Did he smile his work to see?
Did he who made the Lamb make thee?

Tyger! Tyger! burning bright
In the forests of the night,
What immortal hand or eye,
Dare frame thy fearful symmetry?

William Blake

. . . Romance! Those first-class passengers they like it very well,
Printed an' bound in little books; but why don't poets tell?
I'm sick of all their quirks an' turns – the loves an' doves they
    dream –
Lord, send a man like Robbie Burns to sing the Song o' Steam!
To match wi' Scotia's noblest speech yon orchestra sublime
Whaurto – uplifted like the Just – the tail-rods mark the time.

Creation

The crank-throws give the double-bass, the feed-pump sobs an'
  heaves,
An' now the main eccentrics start their quarrel on the sheaves:
Her time, her own appointed time, the rocking link-head bides,
Till – hear that note? – the rod's return whings glimmerin'
  through the guides.
They're all awa'! True beat, full power, the clangin' chorus goes
Clear to the tunnel where they sit, my purrin' dynamoes.
Interdependence absolute, foreseen, ordained, decreed,
To work, ye'll note, at ony tilt an' every rate o' speed.
Fra' skylight-lift to furnace-bars, backed, bolted, braced an'
  stayed,
An' singin' like the Mornin' Stars for joy that they are made;
While, out o' touch o' vanity, the sweating thrust-block says:
'Not unto us the praise, or man – not unto us the praise!'
Now, a'together, hear them lift their lesson, theirs an' mine:
'Law, Orrder, Duty an' Restraint, Obedience, Discipline!'
Mill, forge an' try-pit taught them that when roarin' they arose
An' whiles I wonder if a soul was gied them wi' the blows.
Oh for a man to weld it then, in one trip-hammer strain,
Till even first-class passengers could tell the meaning plain!
But no one cares except mysel' that serve an' understand
My seven thousand horse-power here. Eh, Lord! They're grand –
  they're grand!
Uplift am I? When first in store the new-made beasties stood,
Were Ye cast down that breathed the Word declarin' all things
  good?
Not so! O' that world-liftin' joy no after-fall could vex,
Ye've left a glimmer still to cheer the Man – the Arrtifex!

Rudyard Kipling, 'McAndrew's Hymn'

In Memory of
JANE AUSTEN
youngest daughter of the late
Revd GEORGE AUSTEN
formerly Rector of Steventon in this County
She departed this life on the 18th of July 1817,
aged 41, after a long illness supported with
the patience and the hopes of a Christian.

The benevolence of her heart,
The sweetness of her temper, and
the extraordinary endowments of her mind
obtained the regard of all who knew her, and
the warmest love of her intimate connections.

Their grief is in proportion to their affection
they know their loss to be irreparable,
but in their deepest affliction they are consoled
by a firm though humble hope that her charity,
devotion, faith and purity, have rendered
her soul acceptable in the sight of her
REDEEMER

Jane Austen's Epitaph in Winchester Cathedral

. . . While here I stand, not only with the sense
Of present pleasure, but with pleasing thoughts
That in this moment there is life and food
For future years.

William Wordsworth, 'Lines composed a few miles above Tintern Abbey', ll. 62–5

. . . as one man
In old age plants an avenue of limes

And before they bloom can smell them, before they span
The road can walk beneath the perfected arch,
The merest greenprint when the lives began

Of those who walk there with him . . .

Louis MacNeice, 'A Fanfare for the Makers'

I hope I have not in too late a day touched the beautiful mythology of Greece, and dulled its brightness: for I wish to try once more, before I bid it farewell.

John Keats, Preface to *Endymion*

What good fortune for these insignificant birds to have been painted by this sage.

Metropolitan Museum, New York, Chinese painting of finches 1254–1302

Let Euclid rest and Archimedes pause,
And what the *Swede* intend, and what the *French*.
To measure life, learn thou betimes, and know
Toward solid good what leads the nearest way;
For other things mild Heav'n a time ordains,
And disapproves that care, though wise in show,
That with superfluous burden loads the day,
And when God sends a cheerful hour, refrains.

John Milton, Sonnet: 'Cyriack, whose Grandsire . . .'

Profitable Wonders

The Puritan through life's sweet garden goes
To pluck the thorn and throw away the rose
And hopes to please by this peculiar whim
The God who fashioned it and gave it him.

Kenneth Hare, *Poems 1923*

(I.41) It is very strange; Want itself is a Treasure in Heaven: And so great an one, that without it there could be no Treasure. GOD did infinitly for us, when He made us to Want like GODS, that like GODS we might be satisfied. The Heathen DIETIES wanted nothing, and were therefore unhappy; For they had no Being. But the LORD GOD of Israel the living and true GOD, was from all Eternity, and from all Eternity Wanted like a GOD. He wanted the Communication of His Divine Essence, and Persons to Enjoy it. He wanted Worlds, He wanted Spectators, He wanted Joys, He wanted Treasures. He wanted, yet he wanted not, for he had them.

(I.42) This is very strange that GOD should Want. For in Him is the Fulness of all Blessedness: He overfloweth Eternally. His Wants are as Glorious as infinit. Perfectiv needs that are in His Nature, and ever Blessed, becaus always Satisfied. He is from Eternity full of Want: or els He would not be full of Treasure. Infinit Want is the very Ground and Caus of infinit Treasure. It is Incredible, yet very Plain: Want is the Fountain of all His Fulness. Want in GOD is a Treasure to us. For had there been no Need He would not hav Created the World, nor made us, nor Manifested His Wisdom, nor Exercised his Power, nor Beautified Eternity, nor prepared the Joys of Heaven. But He Wanted Angels and Men, Images, Companions. And these He had from all Eternitie.

(I.44) You must want like a GOD, that you may be satisfied like GOD. Were you not made in His Image?

Thomas Traherne, *Centuries*

(l. 638) I knew, I felt, . . .

. . . – what God is, what we are,
What life is – how God tastes an infinite joy
In infinite ways – one everlasting bliss,
From whom all being emanates, all power
Proceeds; in whom is life for evermore,
Yet whom existence in its lowest form
Includes; where dwells enjoyment there is he:
With still a flying point of bliss remote,
A happiness in store afar, a sphere
Of distant glory in full view; thus climbs
Pleasure its heights for ever and for ever.
The centre-fire heaves underneath the earth,
And the earth changes like a human face;
The molten ore bursts up among the rocks,
Winds into the stone's heart, outbranches bright
In hidden mines, spots barren river-beds,
Crumbles into fine sand where sunbeams bask –
God joys therein. The wroth sea's waves are edged
With foam, white as the bitten lip of hate,
When, in the solitary waste, strange groups
Of young volcanoes come up, cyclops-like,
Staring together with their eyes on flame –
God tastes a pleasure in their uncouth pride.
Then all is still; earth is a wintry clod:
But spring-wind, like a dancing psaltress, passes
Over its breast to waken it, rare verdure
Buds tenderly upon rough banks, between
The withered tree-roots and the cracks of frost,
Like a smile striving with a wrinkled face;
The grass grows bright, the boughs are swoln with blooms
Like chrysalids impatient for the air,
The shining dorrs are busy, beetles run
Along the furrows, ants make their ado;

Above, birds fly in merry flocks, the lark
Soars up and up, shivering for very joy;
Afar the ocean sleeps; white fishing-gulls
Flit where the sound is purple with its tribe
Of nested limpets; savage creatures seek
Their loves in wood and plain – and God renews
His ancient rapture. Thus he dwells in all,
From life's minute beginnings, up at last
To man – the consummation of this scheme
Of being, the completion of this sphere
Of life . . .

Robert Browning, 'Paracelsus' V

And all killing insects and gnawing worms,
And things of obscene and unlovely forms,
She bore, in a basket of Indian woof,
Into the rough woods far aloof, –

In a basket, of grasses and wild-flowers full,
The freshest her gentle hands could pull
For the poor banished insects, whose intent,
Although they did ill, was innocent.

Percy Bysshe Shelley, 'The Sensitive Plant', ll. 41–8

But this change of taste in gardening was to be the beginning and –
I do not, assuredly, say, *the* cause, but the foreshadowing, and one of
the joint causes – of a change of taste in all the arts and, indeed, of a
change of taste in universes. In one of its aspects that many-sided
thing called Romanticism may not inaccurately be described as a
conviction that the world is an *englischer Garten* on a grand scale. The
God of the seventeenth century, like its gardeners, always
geometrized; the God of Romanticism was one in whose universe

things grew wild and without trimming and in all the rich diversity of their natural shapes.

Arthur O. Lovejoy, The Great Chain of Being, pp. 15–16

Even in those who accepted the premise of the optimists that the rationality and excellence of nature consist in its 'fullness', there sometimes broke through a feeling that it would be pleasanter if it were not quite so full.

Arthur O. Lovejoy, The Great Chain of Being, p. 240

The Creator, if He exists, has a special preference for beetles.
(There are fifty times as many species of beetles as species of mammals.)

J. B. S. Haldane, in a lecture given on 7 April 1951, printed in the Journal of the British Interplanetary Society, Vol. 10

In the heat of composition I find that I have inadvertently allowed myself to assume the form of a large centipede.

C. S. Lewis, The Screwtape Letters, 22

'The sweets of housekeeping in a country village!' said Miss Crawford, archly. 'Commend me to the nurseryman and the poulterer.'

Jane Austen, Mansfield Park, Chapter 4

The lot is fallen unto me in a fair ground: yea, I have a goodly heritage.

Psalm 16.7

Profitable Wonders

God gave all men all earth to love,
But, since man's heart is small,
Ordained for each one spot should prove
Belovèd over all;
That, as He watched Creation's birth,
So we, in godlike mood,
May of our love create our earth
And see that it is good.

Rudyard Kipling, 'Sussex'

Then at dawn we came down to a temperate valley,
Wet, below the snowline, smelling of vegetation;

T. S. Eliot, 'Journey of the Magi' (from Lancelot Andrewes)

. . . And we slope to Italy at last
And youth, by green degrees.

Robert Browning, 'By the fireside', V

Kennst du das Land, wo die Zitronen blühn,
Im dunkeln Laub die Gold-Orangen glühn
Ein sanfter Wind vom blauen Himmel weht,
Die Myrte still und hoch der Lorbeer steht?
Kennst du es wohl? – Dahin! Dahin
Möcht ich mit dir, o mein Geliebter, ziehn.

Knowst thou the land where the lemon trees flower,
Where among the dark leaves the gold oranges glow,
Where a soft wind blows from the blue sky,
The myrtle stands quiet and the laurel tall?
Do you really know it? Yonder! Yonder,
O my beloved, would I go with thee.

Johann Wolfgang von Goethe, 'Mignons Lied'

Creation

... He hangs in shades the orange bright,
Like golden lamps in a green night ...

Andrew Marvell, 'Bermudas'

... And the green lizard, and the golden snake,
Like unimprisoned flames, out of their trance awake.

Percy Bysshe Shelley, 'Adonais: an elegy on the death of John Keats', XVIII

Tall are the oaks whose acorns
Drop in dark Auser's rill;
Fat are the stags that champ the boughs
Of the Ciminian hill;
Beyond all streams Clitumnus
Is to the herdsman dear;
Best of all pools the fowler loves
The great Volsinian mere.

Lord Macaulay, Lays of Ancient Rome, 'Horatius', VI

Upon the infinitely sensitive pads of his feet he took the clear stamp
of proud Latin inscriptions.

Virginia Woolf, Flush, p. 124

Mein Auge liess das hohe Meer zurücke,
Als aus der Flut Palladios Tempel stiegen,
An deren Staffeln sich die Wellen schmiegen,
Die uns getragen ohne Falsch und Tücke.

Wir landen an, wir danken es dem Glücke,
Und die Lagune scheint zurück zu fliegen,
Der Dogen alte Säulengänge liegen
Vor uns gigantisch mit der Seufzerbrücke.

[45]

Venedigs Löwen, sonst Venedigs Wonne,
Mit ehrnen Flügeln sehen wir ihn ragen
Auf seiner kolossalischen Kolonne.

Ich steig' ans Land, nicht ohne Furcht und Zagen,
Da glänzt der Markusplatz im Licht der Sonne:
Soll ich ihn wirklich zu betreten wagen?

My gaze was leaving the open sea behind,
As from the water Palladio's temples were rising,
On whose steps the waves beat,
Which have borne us without deceit or betrayal.

We come to land, we return thanks to fortune,
And the lagoon seems to fly back,
The Doge's ancient colonnades lie
Gigantic before us with the Bridge of Sighs.

The Lion of Venice, once the joy of Venice
We see him tower with bronze wings
On his colossal column.

I step ashore, not without fear and hesitation,
There gleams St Mark's Square in the light of the sun:
Shall I really dare to set foot on it?

August Graf von Platen, 'Venedig'/'Venice'

I discovered in Italy that Christ had walked on the earth, and also that things truly made preserve themselves through time in the first freshness of their nature.

Edwin Muir, *An Autobiography*, p. 280

[46]

Creation

... Ere we retired,
The cock had crow'd, the sky was bright with day.
Two miles I had to walk along the fields
Before I reached my home. Magnificent
The morning was, in memorable pomp,
More glorious than I ever had beheld.
The sea was laughing at a distance; all
The solid Mountains were as bright as clouds,
Grain-tinctured, drench'd in empyrean light;
And, in the meadows and the lower grounds,
Was all the sweetness of a common dawn,
Dews, vapours, and the melody of birds,
And Labourers going forth into the fields.
– Ah! need I say, dear Friend, that to the brim
My heart was full; I made no vows, but vows
Were then made for me; bond unknown to me
Was given, that I should be, else sinning greatly,
A dedicated Spirit. On I walked,
In blessedness, which even yet remains.

William Wordsworth, *The Prelude*, IV.327–45

But here is the finger of God, a flash of the will that can,
Existent behind all laws, that made them and, lo, they are!
And I know not if, save in this, such gift be allowed to man,
That out of three sounds he frame, not a fourth sound, but a star.

Robert Browning, 'Abt Vogler', v. VII

From harmony, from heavenly harmony,
This universal frame began:
When nature underneath a heap
Of jarring atoms lay,
And could not heave her head,
The tuneful voice was heard from high,

'Arise, ye more than dead!'
When hot, and cold, and moist, and dry,
In order to their stations leap,
And Music's power obey.
From harmony, from heavenly harmony,
This universal frame began:
From harmony to harmony,
Through all the compass of the notes it ran,
The diapason closing full in Man.

What passion cannot Music raise and quell?
When Jubal struck the chorded shell,
His listening brethren stood around,
And, wondering, on their faces fell
To worship that celestial sound:
Less than a God they thought there could not dwell
Within the hollow of that shell,
That spoke so sweetly, and so well.
What passion cannot Music raise and quell?

The trumpet's loud clangour
Excites us to arms,
With shrill notes of anger,
And mortal alarms.
The double double double beat
Of the thundering drum
Cries Hark! the foes come;
Charge, charge, 'tis too late to retreat!
The soft complaining flute,
In dying notes, discovers
The woes of hopeless lovers,
Whose dirge is whisper'd by the warbling lute.
Sharp violins proclaim
Their jealous songs and desperation,

Fury, frantic indignation,
Depth of pains, and height of passion
For the fair, disdainful dame.
But O, what art can teach,
What human voice can reach,
The sacred organ's praise?
Notes inspiring holy love,
Notes that wing their heavenly ways
To mend the choirs above.
Orpheus could lead the savage race;
And trees uprooted left their place,
Sequacious of the lyre;
But bright Cecilia raised the wonder higher:
When to her organ vocal breath was given,
An angel heard, and straight appear'd
Mistaking earth for Heaven.
   GRAND CHORUS
As from the power of sacred lays
The spheres began to move,
And sung the great Creator's praise
To all the Blest above;
So when the last and dreadful hour
This crumbling pageant shall devour,
The trumpet shall be heard on high,
The dead shall live, the living die,
And Music shall untune the sky!

John Dryden, 'A song for St Cecilia's Day 1687'

. . . And every phrase
And sentence that is right (where every word is at home,
Taking its place to support the others,
The word neither diffident nor ostentatious,
An easy commerce of the old and the new,

The common word exact without vulgarity,
The formal word precise but not pedantic,
The complete consort dancing together) . . .

T. S. Eliot, *Four Quartets*, 'Little Gidding', V

Scorn not the Sonnet; Critic, you have frowned
Mindless of its just honours; with this key
Shakspeare unlocked his heart; the melody
Of this small lute gave ease to Petrarch's wound;
A thousand times this pipe did Tasso sound;
With it Camöens soothed an exile's grief;
The Sonnet glittered a gay myrtle leaf
Amid the cypress with which Dante crowned
His visionary brow: a glow-worm lamp,
It cheered mild Spenser, called from Faery-land
To struggle through dark ways; and when a damp
Fell round the path of Milton, in his hand
The Thing became a trumpet; whence he blew
Soul-animating strains – alas, too few!

William Wordsworth

. . . In truth the prison, unto which we doom
Ourselves, no prison is: and hence for me,
In sundry moods, 'twas pastime to be bound
Within the Sonnet's scanty plot of ground;
Pleased if some souls (for such there needs must be)
Who have felt the weight of too much liberty
Should find brief solace there, as I have found.

William Wordsworth, 'Nuns fret not'

. . . the croquet balls were live hedgehogs, and the mallets live flamingoes, and the soldiers had to double themselves up and stand on their hands and feet, to make the arches . . .

'I don't think they play at all fairly', Alice began, in rather a complaining tone, 'and they all quarrel so dreadfully one can't hear oneself speak – and they don't seem to have any rules in particular: or at least, if there are, nobody attends to them – and you've no idea how confusing it is all the things being alive: for instance, there's the arch I've got to go through next walking about at the other end of the ground – and I should have croqueted the Queen's hedgehog just now, only it ran away when it saw mine coming!'

Lewis Carroll, Alice's Adventures in Wonderland, Chapter 8

'Tis pleasant, sure, to see one's name in print;
A book's a book, although there's nothing in't.

Lord Byron, 'English bards and Scotch reviewers', ll. 51–2

You may crush an artist by telling him that what he has just done may be quite good in its own way, only it is not 'Art'. And you may confound anyone enjoying a picture by declaring that what he liked in it was not the Art but something different.

Actually I do not think that there are any wrong reasons for liking a statue or a picture. Someone may like a landscape painting because it reminds him of home, or a portrait because it reminds him of a friend. There is nothing wrong with that. All of us, when we see a painting, are bound to be reminded of a hundred-and-one things which influence our likes and dislikes. As long as these memories help us to enjoy what we see, we need not worry. It is only when some irrelevant memory makes us prejudiced, when we instinctively turn away from a magnificent picture of an alpine scene because we dislike climbing, that we should search our mind for the reason of the aversion which spoils a pleasure we might otherwise have had. There *are* wrong reasons for disliking a work of art.

. E. H. Gombrich, *The Story of Art*, p. 15

Le mieux est l'ennemi du bien.

The best is the enemy of the good.

Voltaire, *Dictionnaire Philosophique: Art Dramatique*

'I see. Just something about "Better than Butter and half the price?" Simple appeal to the pocket.'

'Yes, but you mustn't knock butter. They sell butter as well.'

'Oh!'

'You can say it's as good as butter.'

'But in that case,' objected Mr Bredon, 'What does one find to say in favour of buying butter? I mean, if the other stuff's as good and doesn't cost so much, what's the argument for buying butter?'

'You don't need an argument for buying butter. It's a natural, human instinct.'

'Oh, I see.'

Dorothy L. Sayers, *Murder Must Advertise*, p. 14

Tax not the royal Saint with vain expense,
With ill-matched aims the Architect who planned –
Albeit labouring for a scanty band
Of white-robed Scholars only – this immense
And glorious work of fine intelligence!
Give all thou canst; high Heaven rejects the lore
Of nicely-calculated less or more;
So deemed the man who fashioned for the sense
These lofty pillars, spread that branching roof

Creation

Self-poised, and scooped into ten thousand cells
Where light and shade repose, where music dwells
Lingering – and wandering on as loth to die:
Like thoughts whose very sweetness yieldeth proof
That they were born for immortality.

William Wordsworth, 'The Inside of King's College Chapel, Cambridge'

Si monumentum requiris, circumspice.

If you would see his monument, look around you.

Christopher Wren's Epitaph in St Paul's Cathedral

O! reason not the need: our basest beggars
Are in the poorest thing superfluous:
Allow not nature more than Nature needs,
Man's life is cheap as beast's.

William Shakespeare, *King Lear*, II.4.264–7

Loving in truth, and fain in verse my love to show,
That she (dear she) might take some pleasure of my pain:
Pleasure might cause her read, reading might make her know,
Knowledge might pity win, and pity grace obtain,
I sought fit words to paint the blackest face of woe,
Studying inventions fine, her wits to entertain:
Oft turning others' leaves, to see if thence would flow
Some fresh and fruitful showers upon my sunburnt brain.
But words came halting forth, wanting Invention's stay,
Invention, Nature's child, fled step-dame Study's blows,
And others' feet still seemed but strangers in my way.
Thus great with child to speak, and helpless in my throes
    Biting my truant pen, beating myself for spite,
    Fool, said my Muse to me, look in thy heart and write.

Philip Sidney

Why do so many writers prefer complexity to simplicity? It seems to be a morbid condition contracted in early manhood. Children show no signs of it. Here, for example, is the response of a child of ten to an invitation to write an essay on a beast and a bird:

The bird that I am going to write about is the owl. The Owl cannot see at all by day and at night is as blind as a bat.

I do not know much about the owl, so I will go on to the beast which I am going to choose. It is the cow. The cow is a mammal. It has six sides – right, left, an upper and below. At the back it has a tail on which hangs a brush. With this it sends the flies away so that they do not fall into the milk. The head is for the purpose of growing horns and so that the mouth can be somewhere. The horns are to butt with, and the mouth is to moo with. Under the cow hangs the milk. It is arranged for milking. When people milk, the milk comes and there is never an end to the supply. How the cow does it I have not yet realised, but it makes more and more. The cow has a fine sense of smell; one can smell it far away. This is the reason for the fresh air in the country.

The man cow is called an ox. It is not a mammal. The cow does not eat much, but what it eats it eats twice, so that it gets enough. When it is hungry it moos, and when it says nothing it is because its inside is all full up with grass.

Ernest Gowers, The Complete Plain Words, pp. 42–3

O praise the Lord of heaven: praise him in the height.
Praise him, all ye angels of his: praise him, all his host.
Praise him, sun and moon: praise him, all ye stars and light.
Praise him, all ye heavens: and ye waters that are above the
    heavens.
Let them praise the Name of the Lord: for he spoke the word, and
    they were made; he commanded, and they were created.
He hath made them fast for ever and ever: he hath given them a
    law which shall not be broken.

Creation

Praise the Lord upon earth: ye dragons, and all deeps;
Fire and hail, snow and vapours: wind and storm, fulfilling his
    word;
Mountains and all hills: fruitful trees and all cedars;
Beasts and all cattle: worms and feathered fowls;
Kings of the earth and all people: princes and all judges of the
    world;
Young men and maidens, old men and children, praise the Name
    of the Lord: for his Name only is excellent, and his praise above
    heaven and earth.
He shall exalt the horn of his people: all his saints shall praise him:
    even the children of Israel, even the people that serveth him.

Psalm 148

... Hail, Snow and Ice that praise the Lord. I've met them at
    their work,
An' wished we had anither route or they anither kirk.

Rudyard Kipling, 'McAndrew's Hymn'

How the lit lake shines, a phosphoric sea,
And the big rain comes dancing to the earth!

Lord Byron, *Childe Harold's Pilgrimage*, III.xciii

Es geht zum Herbst; die Luft wird seltsam blaß,
Die reifen Äpfel fallen dumpf ins Gras,
Die Störche suchten längst den Wanderpfad
Die Nacht wird kalt und Allerseelen naht.
Bald stirbt das Laub, und so kommt eins zum andern.
– Mein lieber Freund, wann müssen wir wohl wandern?

Autumn draws on; the air is strangely pale,
Apples are ripe and fall thud in the grass,

[55]

Profitable Wonders

The storks sought long ago their wandering way
The nights grow cold and Hallowe'en is near.
Soon the leaves die, and everything is changed.
– Now, my dear friend, when must we wander too?

Karl Büsse, 'Herbstbeginn'/ 'The Beginning of Autumn'

Herr, es ist Zeit. Der Sommer war sehr groß.
Leg' deinen Schatten auf die Sonnenuhren
Und auf den Fluren laß die Winde los.

Befiel den letzen Früchten voll zu sein;
Gib ihnen noch zwei südlichere Tage,
Dränge sie zur Vollendung hin und jage
Die letzte Süße in den schweren Wein.

Wer jetzt kein Haus hat, baut sich keines mehr
Wer jetzt allein ist, wird es lange bleiben,
Wird wachen, lesen, lange Briefe schreiben
Und wird in den Alleen hin und her
Unruhig wandern, wenn die Blätter trieben.

Lord, it is time. The summer has been good.
Lay thou thy shadow on the sundials now
And on the meadows let the tempests loose.

Command the last fruits to ripen;
Give them two more southerly days,
Hurry them on to fullness, and force
The final sweetness in the heavy wine.

Who has no house now, he will build no more
Who is alone now, will long so remain,
Will wake, and read, and lengthy letters write,

And in the alleys will go to and fro
Restlessly wandering, while the leaves are falling.

Rainer Maria Rilke, 'Herbsttag'/'Autumn day'

Season of mists and mellow fruitfulness,
Close bosom-friend of the maturing sun,
Conspiring with him how to load and bless
With fruit the vines that round the thatch-eves run:
To bend with apples the mossed cottage trees,
And fill all fruit with ripeness to the core;
To swell the gourd and plump the hazel shells
With a sweet kernel; to set budding more,
And still more, later flowers for the bees,
Until they think warm days will never cease,
For summer has o'erbrimmed their clammy cells.

Who has not seen thee oft amid thy store?
Sometimes whoever seeks abroad may find
Thee sitting careless by a granary floor,
Thy hair soft-lifted by the winnowing wind;
Or on a half-reaped furrow sound asleep,
Drowsed with the fume of poppies, while thy hook
Spares the next swath and all its twinèd flowers;
And sometimes like a gleaner thou dost keep
Steady thy laden head across a brook;
Or by a cyder-press, with patient look,
Thou watchest the last oozings hours by hours.

Where are the songs of spring? Aye, where are they?
Think not of them, thou hast thy music too –
While barrèd clouds bloom the soft-dying day,
And touch the stubble-plains with rosy hue.
Then in a wailful choir the small gnats mourn

Along the river sallows, borne aloft
Or sinking, as the light wind lives or dies;
And full-grown lambs loud bleat from hilly bourn;
Hedge crickets sing; and now with treble soft
The red-breast whistles from a garden-croft
And gathering swallows twitter in the skies.

John Keats, 'To Autumn'

Have you seene but a bright Lillie grow,
  Before rude hands have touch'd it?
Have you mark'd but the fall o' the Snow
  Before the soyle hath smutch'd it?
Have you felt the wooll o' the Bever?
    Or Swan's Downe ever?
Or have smelt o' the bud o' the Brier,
    Or the Nard i' the Fire?
  Or have tasted the bag o' the Bee?
O so white! O so soft! O so sweet is she!

Ben Jonson, 'Her triumph'

(I.27) You never Enjoy the World aright, till you see how a Sand Exhibiteth the Wisdom and Power of God: And prize in evry thing the Service which they do you, by Manifesting His Glory and Goodness to your Soul, far more than the Visible Beauty on their Surface, or the Material Services, they can do your Body. Wine by its Moysture quencheth my Thirst, whether I consider it or no: but to see it flowing from his Lov who gav it unto Man. Quencheth the Thirst even of the Holy Angels. To consider it, is to Drink it Spiritualy. To rejoice in its Diffusion is to be of a Publick Mind. And to take Pleasure in all the Benefits it doth to all is Heavenly. for so they do in Heaven. To do so, is to be Divine and Good. and to imitat our Infinit and Eternal Father.

(I.28) Your Enjoyment of the World is never right, till evry Morning you awake in Heaven: see your self in your fathers Palace: and look upon the Skies and the Earth and the Air, as Celestial Joys: having such a Reverend Esteem of all, as if you were among the Angels. The Bride of a Monarch, in her Husbands Chamber, hath no such Causes of Delight as you.

(I.29) You never Enjoy the World aright, till the Sea it self floweth in your Veins, till you are Clothed with the Heavens, and Crowned with the Stars: and Perceiv your self to be the Sole Heir of the whole World: and more then so, becaus Men are in it who are evry one Sole Heirs, as well as you. Till you can Sing and Rejoyce and Delight in GOD, as Misers do in Gold, and Kings in Scepters, you never enjoy the World.

Thomas Traherne, *Centuries*

I heard a thousand blended notes,
While in a grove I sate reclined,
In that sweet mood when pleasant thoughts
Bring sad thoughts to the mind.

To her fair works did Nature link
The human soul that through me ran;
And much it grieved my heart to think
What man has made of man.

Through primrose tufts, in that green bower,
The periwinkle trailed its wreaths;
And 'tis my faith that every flower
Enjoys the air it breathes.

The birds around me hopped and played,
Their thoughts I cannot measure:–

But the least motion which they made,
It seemed a thrill of pleasure.

The budding leaves spread out their fan,
To catch the breezy air;
And I must think, do all I can,
That there was pleasure there.

If this belief from heaven be sent,
If such be Nature's holy plan,
Have I not reason to lament
What man has made of man?

William Wordsworth, 'Lines written in early Spring'

Here are sweetpeas, on tip-toe for a flight, . . .

Where swarms of minnows show their little heads,
Staying their wavy bodies 'gainst the streams,
To taste the luxury of sunny beams
Tempered with coolness.

John Keats, 'I stood tip-toe upon a little hill', ll. 57, 72–5

Catherine Morland: 'I have just learnt to love a hyacinth.'

Jane Austen, *Northanger Abbey*, Chapter 7

. . . daffodils,
That come before the swallow dares, and take
The winds of March with beauty . . .

William Shakespeare, *The Winter's Tale*, IV.3.118–20

I wandered lonely as a cloud
That floats on high o'er vales and hills,

When all at once I saw a crowd,
A host of golden daffodils;
Beside the lake, beneath the trees,
Fluttering and dancing in the breeze.

Continuous as the stars that shine
And twinkle on the milky way,
They stretched in never-ending line
Along the margin of a bay:
Ten thousand saw I at a glance,
Tossing their heads in sprightly dance.

The waves beside them danced; but they
Outdid the sparkling waves in glee;
A poet could not but be gay,
In such a jocund company:
I gazed – and gazed – but little thought
What wealth the show to me had brought:

For oft, when on my couch I lie
In vacant or in pensive mood,
They flash upon that inward eye
Which is the bliss of solitude;
And then my heart with pleasure fills,
And dances with the daffodils.

William Wordsworth, 'Daffodils'

(l. 215) Or say there's beauty with no soul at all –
          (I never saw it – put the case the same –)
          If you get simple beauty and nought else,
          You get about the best thing God invents:
          That's somewhat: and you'll find the soul you've missed,
          Within yourself, when you return him thanks.

(l. 282) . . . you've seen the world
　　　　　– The beauty and the wonder and the power,
　　　　　The shapes of things, their colours, lights and shades,
　　　　　Changes, surprises, – and God made it all!
　　　　　– For what? Do you feel thankful, aye or no,
　　　　　For this fair town's face, yonder river's line,
　　　　　The mountain round it and the sky above,
　　　　　Much more the figures of man, woman, child,
　　　　　These are the frame to? What's it all about?
　　　　　To be passed over, despised? or dwelt upon,
　　　　　Wondered at? Oh, this last of course! – you say.
　　　　　But why not do as well as say, – paint these
　　　　　Just as they are, careless what comes of it?
　　　　　God's works – paint anyone, and count it crime
　　　　　To let a truth slip. Don't object, 'His works
　　　　　Are here already; nature is complete:
　　　　　Suppose you reproduce her' – (which you can't)
　　　　　'There's no advantage! You must beat her, then.'
　　　　　For, don't you mark? We're made so that we love
　　　　　First when we see them painted, things we have passed
　　　　　Perhaps a hundred times nor cared to see:
　　　　　And so they are better, painted – better to us,
　　　　　Which is the same thing. Art was given for that;
　　　　　God uses us to help each other so,
　　　　　Lending our minds out.

Robert Browning, 'Fra Lippo Lippi'

Beauty is the convenient and traditional name of something which art and nature share, and which gives a fairly clear sense to the idea of quality of experience and change of consciousness. I am looking out of my window in an anxious and resentful state of mind, oblivious of my surroundings, brooding perhaps on some damage done to my prestige. Then suddenly I observe a hovering kestrel. In a moment everything is altered. The brooding self with its hurt vanity has disappeared. There is nothing now but kestrel. And when I return to thinking of the other matter it seems less important. And of course this is something which we may also do deliberately: give attention to nature in order to clear our minds of selfish care. It may seem odd to start the argument against what I have roughly labelled as 'romanticism' by using the case of attention to nature. In fact I do not think that any of the great romantics really believed that we receive but what we give and in our life alone does nature live, although the lesser ones tended to follow Kant's lead and use nature as an occasion for exalted self-feeling. The great romantics, including the one I have just quoted, transcended 'romanticism'. A self-directed enjoyment of nature seems to me to be something forced. More naturally, as well as more properly, we take a self-forgetful pleasure in the sheer alien pointless independent existence of animals, birds, stones and trees. 'Not how the world is, but that it is, is the mystical.'

I take this starting-point, not because I think it is the most important place of moral change, but because I think it is the most accessible one. It is so patently a good thing to take delight in flowers and animals that people who bring home potted plants and watch kestrels might even be surprised at the notion that these things have anything to do with virtue.

Iris Murdoch, *The Sovereignty of Good*, p. 84

– I scarcely remember counting upon any Happiness – I look not for it if it be not in the present hour – nothing startles me beyond the Moment. The setting Sun will always set me to rights – or if a Sparrow come before my Window I take part in its existence and peck about the Gravel.

John Keats, Letter to Benjamin Bailey (22 November 1817)

All things that love the sun are out of doors;
The sky rejoices in the morning's birth;
The grass is bright with rain-drops; on the moors
The hare is running races in her mirth;
And with her feet she from the plashy earth
Raises a mist; that, glittering in the sun,
Runs with her all the way, wherever she doth run.

William Wordsworth, 'Resolution and Independence'

What shall I do with you, O Ephraim?
What shall I do with you, O Judah?
Your love is like a morning cloud, like the dew that goes early away.

Hosea 6.4

Full many a glorious morning have I seen
Flatter the mountain tops with sovereign eye,
Kissing with golden face the meadows green,
Gilding pale streams with heavenly alchemy;
Anon permit the basest clouds to ride
With ugly rack on his celestial face,
And from the forlorn world his visage hide
Stealing unseen to west with his disgrace:
Even so my sun one early morn did shine
With all-triumphant splendour on my brow,
But out alack, he was but one hour mine,
The region cloud hath mask'd him from me now,
    Yet him for this my love no whit disdaineth
    Suns of the world may stain, when heaven's sun staineth.

William Shakespeare, Sonnet 33

... my Thoughts would be deeply Engaged with Enquiries, How the Earth did end? Whether walls did Bound it, or Suddain Precipices ... Whatever I could imagin was inconvenient, and my Reason being Posed was Quickly Wearied ... Little did I think that the Earth was Round, and the World so full of Beauty, Light, and Wisdom. When I saw that, I knew by the Perfection of the Work there was a GOD, and was satisfied, and Rejoyced. People underneath and feilds and flowers with another Sun and another Day Pleased me mightily: but more when I knew it was the same Sun that served them by night, that served us by Day.

Thomas Traherne, *Centuries*, III.17

The day thou gavest, Lord, is ended,
The darkness falls at thy behest;
To thee our morning prayers ascended,
Thy praise shall sanctify our rest.

We thank thee that thy Church unsleeping,
While earth rolls onward into light,
Through all the world her watch is keeping,
And rests not now by day or night.

As o'er each continent and island
The dawn leads on another day,
The voice of prayer is never silent,
Nor dies the strain of praise away.

The sun that bids us rest is waking
Our brethren 'neath the western sky,
And hour by hour fresh lips are making
Thy wondrous doings known on high.

So be it, Lord; thy throne shall never,
Like earth's proud empires, pass away;
Thy Kingdom stands, and grows for ever,
Till all thy creatures own thy sway.

J. Ellerton

The day's grown old; the fainting sun
Hath but a little way to run,
And yet his steeds, with all his skill,
Scarce lug the chariot down the hill.

The shadows now so long do grow,
That brambles like tall cedars show;
Mole hills seem mountains, and the ant
Appears a monstrous elephant.

A very little, little flock
Shades thrice the ground that it would stock;
Whilst the small stripling following them
Appears a mighty Polypheme.

And now on benches all are sat,
In the cool air to sit and chat,
Till Phoebus, dipping in the West
Doth lead the world the way to rest.

Charles Cotton

The heavens declare the glory of God: and the firmament showeth
   his handywork.
One day telleth another: and one night certifieth another.
There is neither speech nor language: but their voices are heard
   among them.

Their sound is gone out into all lands: and their words into the ends of the world.

In them hath he set a tabernacle for the sun: which cometh forth as a bridegroom out of his chamber, and rejoiceth as a giant to run his course.

It goeth forth from the uttermost part of the heaven, and runneth about unto the end of it again: and there is nothing hid from the heat thereof.

The law of the Lord is an undefiled law, converting the soul: the testimony of the Lord is sure, and giveth wisdom unto the simple.

The statutes of the Lord are right, and rejoice the heart: the commandment of the Lord is pure, and giveth light unto the eyes.

The fear of the Lord is clean, and endureth for ever: the judgements of the Lord are true, and righteous altogether.

More to be desired are they than gold, yea than much fine gold: sweeter also than honey, and the honeycomb.

Moreover, by them is thy servant taught, and in keeping of them there is great reward.

Who can tell how oft he offendeth: O cleanse thou me from my secret faults.

Keep thy servant also from presumptuous sins, lest they get the dominion over me: so shall I be undefiled, and innocent from the great offence.

Let the words of my mouth, and the meditation of my heart, be alway acceptable in thy sight,

O Lord: my strength, and my redeemer.

Psalm 19

Humanity: glories and inconsistencies

Some diverse opinions about human beings are set alongside one another here. If sinfulness were the whole truth about people, their Creator would hardly be glorious. We may look with delight at people's achievements and with affection at their foibles, in the hope that this is how God the Father sees the human family.

'Modern times' have no monopoly of either peril or promise. Suppose since Darwin we think of ourselves as a sort of animal, as well we may, that need not entail thinking worse of ourselves, but learning to appreciate ourselves and our fellow creatures more. There are diversities of gifts; among which human beings are notably endowed with the gift of language.

If we dare to think ourselves worth saving, the glory of humanity is more than a dream of what might have been. It is a destiny still to be realised, in which the value of each individual person is to be fulfilled.

The world is charged with the grandeur of God.
It will flame out, like shining from shook foil;
It gathers to a greatness, like the ooze of oil
Crushed. Why do men then now not reck his rod?
Generations have trod, have trod, have trod;
And all is seared with trade; bleared, smeared with toil;
And wears man's smudge and shares man's smell: the soil
Is bare now, nor can foot feel, being shod.

And for all this, nature is never spent;
There lives the dearest freshness deep down things;
And though the last lights off the black West went
Oh, morning at the brown brink eastward, springs –
Because the Holy Ghost over the bent
World broods with warm breast and with ah! bright wings.

Gerard Manley Hopkins, 'God's grandeur'

O Lord our Governor, how excellent is thy Name in all the world:
thou that hast set thy glory above the heavens!
Out of the mouth of very babes and sucklings hast thou ordained
strength, because of thine enemies: that thou mightest still the
enemy, and the avenger.
For I will consider thy heavens, even the works of thy fingers: the
moon and the stars, which thou hast ordained.
What is man, that thou art mindful of him, and the son of man,
that thou visitest him?
Thou madest him lower than the angels: to crown him with glory
and worship.
Thou madest him to have dominion of the works of thy hands: and
thou hast put all things in subjection under his feet;
All sheep and oxen: yea and the beasts of the field;
The fowls of the air, and the fishes of the sea: and whatsoever
walketh through the paths of the seas.
O Lord our Governor: how excellent is thy Name in all the world!

Psalm 8

Hamlet: What a piece of work is a man! How noble in reason! How
infinite in faculty! in form, in motion, how express and
admirable! in action how like an angel! in apprehension
how like a god! the beauty of the world! the paragon of
animals! And yet, to me, what is this quintessence of dust?

William Shakespeare, *Hamlet*, II.2.309

Profitable Wonders

Isabella: ... but man, proud man,
Drest in a little brief authority
Most ignorant of what he's most assured
His glassy essence, like an angry ape,
Plays such fantastic tricks before high heaven
As makes the angels weep.

William Shakespeare, *Measure for Measure*, II.2.117–22

O born in days when wits were fresh and clear,
And life ran gaily as the sparkling Thames;
Before this strange disease of modern life,
With its sick hurry, its divided aims,
Its heads o'ertaxed, its palsied hearts, was rife –
Fly hence, our contact fear!

Matthew Arnold, 'The Scholar Gipsy', ll. 201–7 (1853)

Shepherd: I would there were no age between sixteen and three-and-twenty, or that youth would sleep out the rest; for there is nothing in the between but getting wenches with child, wronging the ancientry, stealing, fighting.

William Shakespeare, *The Winter's Tale*, III.3.58

... the utterly memorable struggle between the Cavaliers (Wrong but Wromantic) and the Roundheads (Right but Repulsive).

W. C. Sellar and R. J. Yeatman, *1066 and All That*, p. 63

'And every body praised the Duke
Who this great fight did win.'
'But what good came of it at last?'
Quoth little Peterkin:–

'Why that I cannot tell', said he,
But 'twas a famous victory.'

Robert Southey, 'After Blenheim'

Great Chatham with his sabre drawn
Stood waiting for Sir Richard Strachan.
Sir Richard, longing to be at 'em
Stood waiting for the Earl of Chatham.

Anonymous

Elinor agreed with it all, for she did not think he deserved the compliment of rational opposition.

Jane Austen, *Sense and Sensibility*, Chapter 14

'Well, in *our* country', said Alice, still panting a little, 'you'd generally get to somewhere else – if you ran very fast for a long time as we've been doing.'
   'A slow sort of country!' said the Queen. 'Now, *here* you see, it takes all the running *you* can do, to keep in the same place. If you want to get to somewhere else, you must run at least twice as fast as that!'

Lewis Carroll, *Through the Looking Glass*, Chapter 2

. . . quando la nuova gente alzò la fronte
   ver noi, dicendo a noi: 'se voi sapete,
   mostratene la via di gire al monte.'

E Virgilio rispose, 'Voi credete
   forse che siamo esperti d'este loco;
   ma noi siam peregrin, come voi siete.'

... when the new people lifted up their faces towards us, saying to us, 'If ye know, show us the way to go to the mount.' And Virgil answered, 'Ye think perchance that we have experience of this place, but we are strangers even as ye are.'

Dante Alighieri, *Purgatorio*, II.58–63

Action, after all, is a very difficult thing. The normal acts of our lives are either habitual or compulsory.

Charles Williams, *The English Poetic Mind*, p. 72

Lydia – 'Look here, I have bought this bonnet. I do not think it is very pretty; but I thought I might as well buy it as not. I shall pull it to pieces as soon as I get home, and see if I can make it up any better.'
And when her sisters abused it as ugly, she added, with perfect unconcern, 'Oh! but there were two or three much uglier in the shop; ...'

Jane Austen, *Pride and Prejudice*, Chapter 6

It is astonishing what foolish things one can temporarily believe if one thinks too long alone.

J. M. Keynes, *The General Theory of Employment, Interest and Money*, Preface, p. xxiii

... dreaming of systems so perfect that no one will need to be good.

T. S. Eliot, *The Rock*, VI

But a Christian must not be either a Totalitarian or an Individualist.
I feel a strong desire to tell you – and I expect you feel a strong desire to tell me – which of these two errors is the worst. That is the devil getting at us. He always sends errors into the world in pairs –

pairs of opposites. And he always encourages us to spend a lot of time thinking which is the worse.

C. S. Lewis, *Mere Christianity*, p. 147

The common problem, yours, mine, every one's,
Is – not to fancy what were fair in life
Provided it could be, – but finding first
What may be, then find how to make it fair
Up to our means: a very different thing!

I would have brought my Jerome, frame and all!

Robert Browning, 'Bishop Blougram's Apology', ll. 87–91, 140

Stop and consider! Life is but a day;
A fragile dew-drop on its perilous way
From a tree's summit; a poor Indian's sleep
While his boat hastens to the monstrous steep
Of Montmorenci. Why so sad a moan?
Life is the rose's hope while yet unblown;
The reading of an ever-changing tale;
The light uplifting of a maiden's veil;
A pigeon tumbling in clear summer air;
A laughing school-boy, without grief or care,
Riding the springy branches of an elm.

Oh for ten years, that I may overwhelm
Myself in poesy; so I may do the deed
That my own soul has to itself decreed . . .

And can I ever bid these joys farewell?
Yes, I must pass them for a nobler life,
Where I may find the agonies, the strife
Of human hearts . . .

John Keats, 'Sleep and Poetry', ll.85–98, 122–5

Like as the waves make towards the pebbled shore,
So do our minutes hasten to their end;
Each changing place with that which goes before,
In sequent toil all forwards do contend.
Nativity, once in the main of light,
Crawls to maturity, wherewith being crown'd,
Crooked eclipses 'gainst his glory fight,
And time that gave doth now his gift confound.
Time doth transfix the flourish set on youth
And delves the parallels in beauty's brow,
Feeds on the rarities of nature's truth,
And nothing stands but for his scythe to mow:
    And yet to times in hope my verse shall stand,
    Praising thy worth, despite his cruel hand.

William Shakespeare, Sonnet 60

Ah, did you once see Shelley plain,
And did he stop and speak to you
And did you speak to him again?
How strange it seems and new!

Robert Browning, 'Memorabilia'

If I have given you delight
By aught that I have done
Let me lie quiet in that night
Which shall be yours anon:

And for the little, little span
The dead are borne in mind,
Seek not to question other than
The books I leave behind.

Rudyard Kipling, 'The Appeal'

[74]

Humanity

And you, my midnight darlings, my Folios! Must I part with the intense delight of having you (huge armfuls) in my embraces? Must knowledge come to me, if it come at all, by some awkward process of intuition, and not by the familiar process of reading?

Charles Lamb, *Essays of Elia*, 'New Year's Eve'

Take with you words, and return to the Lord.

Hosea 14.2

They do not live in the world,
Are not in time or space.
From birth to death hurled
No word do they have, not one,
To plant a foot upon,
Were never in any place.

For with names the world was called
Out of the empty air,
With names was built and walled,
Line and circle and square,
Dust and emerald;
Snatched from deceiving death
By the articulate breath.

But these have never trod
Twice the familiar track
Never never turned back
Into the memoried day.
All is new and near
In the unchanging Here
Of the fifth day of God,

That shall remain the same,
Never never pass away.

On the sixth day we came.

Edwin Muir, 'The Animals'

The question is not, Can they reason? nor Can they talk? but Can they suffer?

Jeremy Bentham, *Introduction to the Principles of Morals and Legislation*, Chapter 17 (footnote)

If we are to compare the basic elements of human social life with those of any other species, we need to use analogies, because many of the functions these elements serve simply are not served in any other primate species. Primates do not have big cooperative enterprises, nor therefore the loyalty, fidelity, and developed skills that go with them. Nor do they have fixed homes and families. But the hunting carnivores do. And neither apes nor wolves have anything like the human length of life, nor therefore the same chance of accumulating wisdom and deepening relationships. But elephants do. And no mammal really shares the strong visual interest that is so important both to our social life and to our art, nor perhaps needs to work as hard as we do to rear our young. But birds do. This is why it is vacuous to talk of 'the difference between man and animal' without saying *which* animal.

Mary Midgley, *Beast and Man: The Roots of Human Nature*, p. 335

. . . when my teacher, Oskar Heinroth, described . . . the lifelong, unconditional marital fidelity of the greylag goose as its 'normal' behaviour, he had correctly abstracted the ideal, interference-free type . . . Shortly before writing this chapter I was working with Helga Fischer through her goose records . . . and . . . I evidently showed disappointment that Heinroth's type of perfect goose marriage, faithful unto death, was so rarely to be found among our many geese. Whereupon Helga, exasperated by my disappointment, made the immortal remark, 'What do you expect? After all, geese are only human!'

Konrad Lorenz, On Aggression, p. 167

Consider the auk:
Becoming extinct because he forgot how to fly and could only
    walk.
Consider man, who may well become extinct
Because he forgot how to walk and learned how to fly before he
    thinked.

Ogden Nash, 'A Caution to Everybody'

Clown: What is the opinion of Pythagoras concerning wild fowl?
Malvolio: That the soul of our grandam might haply inhabit a bird.
Clown: What thinkest thou of his opinion?
Malvolio: I think nobly of the soul, and in no way approve his opinion.

William Shakespeare, Twelfth Night, IV.2

Homo sum: humani nil a me alienum puto.

I am a human being: I count nothing human foreign to me.

Terence, Heauton Timoroumenos 77

I saw an aged Beggar in my walk;
And he was seated, by the highway side,
On a low structure of rude masonry
Built at the foot of a huge hill, that they

[77]

Who lead their horses down the steep rough road
May thence remount at ease. The aged Man
Had placed his staff across the broad smooth stone
That overlays the pile; and, from a bag
All white with flour, the dole of village dames,
He drew his scraps and fragments, one by one;
And scanned them with a fixed and serious look
Of idle computation. In the sun,
Upon the second step of that small pile,
Surrounded by those wild unpeopled hills,
He sat, and ate his food in solitude:
And ever, scattered from his palsied hand,
That, still attempting to prevent the waste,
Was baffled still, the crumbs in little showers
Fell on the ground; and the small mountain birds,
Not venturing yet to peck their destined meal,
Approached within the length of half his staff.

Him from my childhood have I known; and then
He was so old, he seems not older now;
He travels on, a solitary Man,
So helpless in appearance, that for him
The sauntering Horseman throws not with a slack
And careless hand his alms upon the ground,
But stops, – that he may safely lodge the coin
Within the old Man's hat; nor quits him so,
But still, when he has given his horse the rein,
Watches the aged Beggar with a look
Sidelong, and half-reverted. She who tends
The toll-gate, when in summer at her door
She turns her wheel, if on the road she sees
The aged Beggar coming, quits her work,
And lifts the latch for him that he may pass.
The post-boy, when his rattling wheels o'ertake

Humanity

The aged Beggar in the woody lane,
Shouts to him from behind; and, if thus warned
The old man does not change his course, the boy
Turns with less noisy wheels to the roadside,
And passes gently by, without a curse
Upon his lips or anger at his heart.

He travels on, a solitary Man;
His age has no companion. On the ground
His eyes are turned, and, as he moves along,
They move along the ground; and, evermore,
Instead of common and habitual sight
Of fields with rural works, of hill and dale,
And the blue sky, one little span of earth
Is all his prospect. Thus, from day to day,
Bow-bent, his eyes for ever on the ground,
He plies his weary journey; seeing still,
And seldom knowing what he sees, some straw,
Some scattered leaf, or marks which, in one track,
The nails of cart or chariot-wheel have left
Impressed on the white road, – in the same line,
At distance still the same. Poor Traveller!
His staff trails with him; scarcely do his feet
Disturb the summer dust; he is so still
In look and motion, that the cottage curs,
Ere he has passed the door, will turn away,
Weary of barking at him. Boys and girls,
The vacant and the busy, maids and youths,
The urchins newly breeched – all pass him by:
Him even the slow-paced waggon leaves behind.

But deem not this Man useless – Statesmen! ye
Who are so restless in your wisdom, ye
Who have a broom still ready in your hands

To rid the world of nuisances; ye proud,
Heart-swoln, while in your pride ye contemplate
Your talents, power, or wisdom, deem him not
A burthen of the earth! 'Tis Nature's law
That none, the meanest of created things,
Of form created the most vile and brute,
The dullest or most noxious, should exist
Divorced from good – a spirit and pulse of good,
A life and soul, to every mode of being
Inseparably linked. Then be assured
That least of all can aught – that ever owned
The heaven-regarding eye and front sublime
Which man is born to – sink, howe'er depressed,
So low as to be scorned without a sin;
Without offence to God cast out of view;
Like the dry remnant of a garden-flower
Whose seeds are shed, or as an implement
Worn out and worthless. While from door to door,
This old Man creeps, the villagers in him.
Behold a record which together binds
Past deeds and offices of charity
Else unremembered, and so keeps alive
The kindly mood in hearts which lapse of years,
And that half-wisdom half-experience gives,
Make slow to feel, and by sure steps resign
To selfishness and cold oblivious cares.
Among the farm and solitary huts,
Hamlets and thinly-scattered villages,
Where'er the aged Beggar takes his rounds,
The mild necessity of use compels
To acts of love; and habit does the work
Of reason; yet prepares that after-joy
Which reason cherishes. And thus the soul,
By that sweet taste of pleasure unpursued,

Doth find herself insensibly disposed
To virtue and true goodness. Some there are,
By their good works exalted, lofty minds,
And meditative, authors of delight
And happiness, which to the end of time
Will live, and spread, and kindle: even such minds
In childhood, from this solitary Being,
Or from like wanderer, haply have received
(A thing more precious far than all that books
Or the solicitudes of love can do!)
That first mild touch of sympathy and thought,
In which they found their kindred with a world
Where want and sorrow were. The easy man
Who sits at his own door, – and, like the pear
That overhangs his head from the green wall,
Feeds in the sunshine; the robust and young,
The prosperous and unthinking, they who live
Sheltered, and flourish in a little grove
Of their own kindred; all behold in him
A silent monitor, which on their minds
Must needs impress a transitory thought
Of self-congratulation, to the heart
Of each recalling his peculiar boons,
His charters and exemptions; and, perchance,
Though he to no one give the fortitude
And circumspection needful to preserve
His present blessings, and to husband up
The respite of the season, he, at least,
And 'tis no vulgar service, makes them felt.

Yet further – Many, I believe, there are
Who live a life of virtuous decency,
Men who can hear the Decalogue and feel
No self-reproach; who of the moral law

[81]

Established in the land where they abide
Are strict observers; and not negligent
In acts of love to those with whom they dwell,
Their kindred, and the children of their blood.
Praise be to such, and to their slumbers peace!
– But of the poor man ask, the abject poor;
Go, and demand of him, if there be here
In this cold abstinence from evil deeds,
And these inevitable charities,
Wherewith to satisfy the human soul?
No – man is dear to man; the poorest poor
Long for some moments in a weary life
When they can know and feel that they have been,
Themselves, the fathers and the dealers-out
Of some small blessings; have been kind to such
As needed kindness, for this single cause
That we have all of us one human heart.
– Such pleasure is to one kind Being known,
My neighbour, when with punctual care, each week,
Duly as Friday comes, though pressed herself
By her own wants, she from her store of meal
Takes one unsparing handful for the scrip
Of this old Mendicant, and, from her door
Returning with exhilarated heart,
Sits by her fire, and builds her hope in heaven.

Then let him pass, a blessing on his head!
And while in that vast solitude to which
The tide of things has borne him, he appears
To breathe and live but for himself alone,
Unblamed, uninjured, let him bear about
The good which the benignant law of Heaven
Has hung around him: and, while life is his,
Still let him prompt the unlettered villagers

To tender offices and pensive thoughts.
– Then let him pass, a blessing on his head!
And, long as he can wander, let him breathe
The freshness of the valleys; let his blood
Struggle with frosty air and winter snows;
And let the chartered wind that sweeps the heath
Beat his grey locks against his withered face.
Reverence the hope whose vital anxiousness
Gives the last human interest to his heart.
May never HOUSE, misnamed of INDUSTRY,
Make him a captive! – for that pent-up din,
Those life-consuming sounds that cloy the air,
Be his the natural silence of old age!
Let him be free of mountain solitudes;
And have around him, whether heard or not,
The pleasant melody of woodland birds.
Few are his pleasures: if his eyes have now
Been doomed so long to settle upon earth
That not without some effort they behold
The countenance of the horizontal sun,
Rising or setting, let the light at least
Find a free entrance to their languid orbs,
And let him, *where* and *when* he will, sit down
Beneath the trees, or on a grassy bank
Of highway side, and with the little birds
Share his chance-gathered meal; and, finally,
As in the eye of Nature he has lived,
So in the eye of Nature let him die!

William Wordsworth, 'The Old Cumberland Beggar'

Whoever be the man that is presented to you as needing your assis-
tance, you have no ground for declining to give it to him. Say he is a
stranger. The Lord has given him a mark which ought to be familiar

to you. Say he is mean and of no consideration. The Lord points him out as one whom he has distinguished by the lustre of his own image. If he not only merits no good, but has provoked you by ignorance and mischief, still this is no good reason why you should not embrace him in love, and visit him with offices of love. He has deserved very differently from me, you will say. But what has the Lord deserved? In this way only we attain to what is not to say difficult, but altogether against nature, to love those that hate us, render good for evil, and blessing for cursing, remembering that we are not to reflect on the wickedness of men, but look for the image of God in them.

John Calvin, *Institutes of the Christian Religion*, III.vii

– There may be intelligences or sparks of the divinity in millions – but they are not Souls till they acquire identities, till each one is personally itself . . . How then are souls to be made? How then are these sparks which are God to have identity given them – so as ever to possess a bliss peculiar to each one's individual existence? How, but by the medium of a world like this?

John Keats, Letter to George and Georgiana Keats, April 1819

. . . the boat, allowing for the usual Malacandrian height and flimsiness, was really very like an earthly boat; only later did he set himself the question, 'What else could a boat be like?'

C. S. Lewis, *Out of the Silent Planet* (Mars), p. 64

Then, little by little, I realised where I was and wished to tell my wishes to those who might satisfy them, but I could not! For my wants were inside me, and they were outside and they could not by any powers of theirs come into my soul. So I would fling my arms and legs about and cry, making the few and feeble gestures that I could, though indeed the signs were not much like what I inwardly

[84]

desired and when I was not satisfied – either from not being understood or because I got what was not good for me – I grew indignant
that my elders were not subject to me and that those on whom I actually had no claim did not wait on me as slaves – and I avenged myself
on them by crying. That infants are like this I have myself been able
to learn by watching them; and they, although they knew me not,
have shown me better what I was like than my own nurses who
knew me.

St Augustine, *Confessions*, I.6

Antiquity! thou wondrous charm, what art thou? that, being nothing, art everything! When thou *wert*, thou wert not antiquity – then
thou wert nothing, but hadst a remoter *antiquity*, as thou calledst it,
to look back to with blind veneration . . . What were thy *dark ages?*
Surely the sun rose as bright then as now, and man got him to his
work in the morning.

Charles Lamb, *Essays of Elia*, 'Oxford in the Vacation'

With five weapons shall we keep our land, with sword and with
shield, with spade and with fork and with the spear, out with the ebb,
up with the flood, to fight day and night against the North-king and
against the wild Viking, that all Frisians shall be free, the born and
the unborn, as long as the wind from the clouds shall blow and the
world shall stand.

Johan Van Veen, 'Dredge drain reclaim' (An ancient Frisian oath)

O Eternal Lord God, who alone spreadest out the heavens, and rulest
the raging of the sea; who hast compassed the waters with bounds
until day and night come to an end; Be pleased to receive into thy
Almighty and most gracious protection the persons of us thy servants and the Fleet in which we serve. Preserve us from the dangers
of the sea, and from the violence of the enemy; that we may be a

safeguard unto our most gracious Sovereign Lady Queen ELIZA-
BETH and her Dominions, and a security for such as pass on the
seas upon their lawful occasions; that the inhabitants of our Island
may in peace and quietness serve thee our God; and that we may
return in safety to enjoy the blessings of the land, with the fruits of
our labours, and with a thankful remembrance of thy mercies to
praise and glorify thy holy Name; through Jesus Christ our Lord.

The Book of Common Prayer, The prayer of the Royal Navy

Another year! – another deadly blow!
Another mighty Empire overthrown!
And We are left, or shall be left, alone;
The last that dare to struggle with the Foe.
'Tis well! from this day forward we shall know
That in ourselves our safety must be sought;
That by our own right hands it must be wrought;
That we must stand unpropped, or be laid low.
O dastard whom such foretaste doth not cheer!
We shall exult, if they who rule the land
Be men who hold its many blessings dear,
Wise, upright, valiant; not a servile band,
Who are to judge of danger which they fear,
And honour which they do not understand.

William Wordsworth, 'November 1806'

I grieved for Buonaparté, with a vain
And an unthinking grief! The tenderest mood
Of that Man's mind – what can it be? What food
Fed his first hopes? What knowledge could *he* gain?
'Tis not in battles that from youth we train
The Governor who must be wise and good,
And temper with the sternness of the brain

[86]

Thoughts motherly, and meek as womanhood.
Wisdom doth live with children round her knees:
Books, leisure, perfect freedom, and the talk
Man holds with week-day man in the hourly walk
Of the mind's business: these are the degrees
By which true Sway doth Mount: this is the stalk
True Power doth grow on; and her rights are these.

William Wordsworth

Alas! What boots it with incessant care
To tend the homely slighted Shepherds trade,
And strictly meditate the thankles Muse,
Were it not better don as others use,
To sport with *Amaryllis* in the shade,
Or with the tangles of *Neaera*'s hair?
Fame is the spur that the clear spirit doth raise
(That last infirmity of Noble mind)
To scorn delights, and live laborious dayes;
But the fair Guerdon when we hope to find,
And think to burst out into sudden blaze,
Comes the blind *Fury* with th' abhorred shears,
And slits the thin spun life. But not the praise,
Phoebus repli'd, and touch'd my trembling ears;
Fame is no plant that grows on mortal soil,
Nor in the glistering foil
Set off to th'world, nor in broad rumour lies,
But lives and spreds aloft by those pure eyes,
And perfect witnes of all judging *Jove*;
As he pronounces lastly on each deed,
Of so much fame in Heav'n expect thy meed.

John Milton, *Lycidas*, ll. 64–84

Ambrose himself I esteemed a happy man, as the world counts happiness, because great personages held him in honour. Only his celibacy appeared to me a painful burden. But what hope he cherished, what struggles he had against the temptations which beset his high station, what solace in adversity, and what savory joys thy bread possessed in the hidden mouth of his heart when feeding upon it, I could neither conjecture nor experience.

Nor did he know my own frustrations, nor the pit of my danger. For I could not request of him what I wanted as I wanted it, because I was debarred from hearing and speaking to him by crowds of busy people to whose infirmities he devoted himself. And when he was not engaged with them – which was never for long at a time – he was either refreshing his body with necessary food or his mind with reading.

Now, as he read, his eyes glanced over the pages and his heart searched out the sense, but his voice and his tongue were silent. Often when we came to his room – for no one was forbidden to enter, nor was it his custom that the arrival of visitors should be announced to him – we would find him thus reading to himself. After we had sat for a long time in silence – for who would dare interrupt one so intent? – we would then depart, realising that he was unwilling to be distracted in the little time he could gain for the recruiting of his mind, free from the clamor of other men's business. Perhaps he was fearful lest, if the author he was studying should express himself vaguely, some doubtful and attentive hearer would ask him to expound it or discuss some of the more abstruse questions, so that he could not get over as much material as he wished, if his time was occupied with others. And even a truer reason for his reading to himself might have been the care for his voice, which was very easily weakened. Whatever his motive in so doing, it was doubtless, in such a man, a good one.

St Augustine, *Confessions*, VI.3

I implore you, good Jesus, that as in your mercy you have given me to drink in with delight the words of your knowledge, so of your loving kindness you will also grant me one day to come to you, the fountain of all wisdom, and to stand for ever before your face.

The Venerable Bede (inscribed in Durham Cathedral)

Hamlet: Sure he that made us with such large discourse,
Looking before and after, gave us not
That capability and god-like reason
To fust in us unused.

William Shakespeare, *Hamlet*, IV.4

Destroy it not; for a blessing is in it.

Isaiah 65.8 (Third Isaiah) (King James Version)

Your Enjoyment is never right, till you esteem evry Soul so great a Treasure as our Savior doth: and that the Laws of God are sweeter than the Hony and Hony Comb becaus they command you to lov them all in such Perfect Maner. For how are they Gods Treasures? Are they not the Riches of his Lov? Is it not his Goodness that maketh Him Glorious to them? Can the Sun or stars serv Him any other Way, then by serving them? And how will you be the Son of God, but by having a Great soul like unto your Fathers. *The Laws of God command you to live in His Image. And to do so, is to live in Heaven.* God commandeth you to lov all like Him, becaus He would have you to be His Son, all them to be your Riches, you to be Glorious before them, and all the Creatures in serving them to be your Treasures, while you are His Delight, like Him in Beauty, and the Darling of His Bosom.

Thomas Traherne, *Centuries*, I.39

He bought thee not with his wealth but with himself. With his own blood he bought thee and redeemed thee. See what right he has over thee, and behold how precious thou art . . . Thou art greater than heaven, thou art greater than the world; of whom the Creator of the world is himself become the price.

Peter Abelard, Letter V

> *My Master*, shall I speak? O that to thee
> *My servant* were a little so,
>   As flesh may be;
> That these two words might creep & grow
> To some degree of spiciness to thee!

George Herbert, 'The Odour' (2 Corinthians 2.15)

He that hath an ear, let him hear what the Spirit saith unto the churches; To him that overcometh will I give to eat of the hidden manna, and will give him a white stone, and in the stone a new name written, which no man knoweth save him that receiveth it.

Revelation 2.17 (King James Version)

Suppose a Curious and fair Woman. Som have seen the Beauties of Heaven, in such a Person. It is a vain thing to say they loved too much. I dare say there are 10000 Beauties in that Creature which they hav not seen. They loved it not too much but upon fals causes. Nor so much upon fals ones, as only upon som little ones. They lov a Creature for Sparkling Eys and Curled Hair, Lillie Brests and Ruddy Cheeks; which they should love moreover for being GODs Image, Queen of the Univers, Beloved by Angels, redeemed by Jesus Christ, an Heiress of Heaven, and Temple of the H. Ghost: a Mine and fountain of all Vertues, a Treasurie of Graces, and a Child of GOD. But these Excellencies are unknown. They lov her perhaps, but do not lov God more: nor Men as much: nor Heaven and Earth at all. And so being Defectiv to other Things; perish by a seeming Excesse to that. We should be all Life and Mettle and Vigor and Lov to evry Thing. And that would Poys us. I dare confidently say, that evry Person in the Whole World ought to be Beloved as much as this: And she if there be any caus of Difference more then she is. But GOD being Beloved infinitly more, will be infinitly more our Joy, and our Heart will be more with Him. So that no Man can be in Danger of loving others too much, that loveth GOD as He ought.

Thomas Traherne, *Centuries*, II.68

. . . All I could never be,
   All, men ignored in me,
This, I was worth to God, whose wheel the pitcher shaped.

   Ay, note that Potter's wheel,
   That metaphor! and feel
Why time spins fast, why passive lies our clay, –
   Thou, to whom fools propound,
   When the wine makes its round,
'Since life fleets, all is change; the Past gone, seize today!'

   Fool! All that is, at all,
   Lasts ever, past recall;
Earth changes, but thy soul and God stand sure:
   What entered into thee,
   That was, is, and shall be:
Time's wheel runs back or stops: Potter and clay endure.

   He fixed thee mid this dance
   Of plastic circumstance,
This Present, thou, forsooth, wouldst fain arrest:
   Machinery just meant
   To give thy soul its bent,
Try thee and turn thee forth, sufficiently impressed.

What though the earlier grooves
Which ran the laughing loves
Around thy base, no longer pause and press?
What though, about thy rim,
Scull-things in order grim
Grow out, in graver mood, obey the sterner stress?

Look thou not down but up!
To uses of a cup,
The festal board, lamp's flash and trumpet's peal,
The new wine's foaming flow,
The Master's lips a-glow!
Thou, heaven's consummate cup, what need'st thou with earth's
wheel?

But I need, now as then,
Thee, God, who mouldest men;
And since, not even while the whirl was worst,
Did I, – to the wheel of life
With shapes and colours rife,
Bound dizzily, – mistake my end, to slake Thy thirst:

So, take and use Thy work:
Amend what flaws may lurk,
What strain o' the stuff, what warpings past the aim!
My times be in Thy hand!
Perfect the cup as planned!
Let age approve of youth, and death complete the same!

Robert Browning, 'Rabbi Ben Ezra', XXV

I opened my mouth, and drew in my breath: for my delight was in
thy commandments.

Psalm 119.131

Humanity

And he said to me, 'Son of man, stand upon your feet, and I will speak with you.'

Ezekiel 2.1

Thou hast made me, and shall thy work decay?
Repair me now, for now mine end doth haste;
I run to death, and death meets me as fast,
And all my pleasures are like yesterday.
I dare not move my dim eyes any way;
Despair behind, and death before doth cast
Such terror, and my feebled flesh doth waste
By sin in it, which it towards hell doth weigh.
Only thou art alone, and when towards thee
By thy leave I can look, I rise again;
But our old subtle foe so tempteth me
That not one hour I can myself sustain.
Thy grace may wing me to prevent his art
And thou like adamant draw mine iron heart.

John Donne

O Lord, thou hast searched me out and known me: thou knowest
  my down-sitting, and mine up-rising; thou understandest my
  thoughts long before.
Thou art about my path, and about my bed: and spiest out all my
  ways. For lo, there is not a word in my tongue: but thou, O Lord,
  knowest it altogether.
Thou hast fashioned me behind and before: and laid thine hand
  upon me.
Such knowledge is too wonderful and excellent for me: I cannot
  attain unto it.
Whither shall I go then from thy Spirit: or whither shall I go then
  from thy presence?

If I climb up into heaven, thou art there: if I go down into hell, thou
art there also.

If I take the wings of the morning: and remain in the uttermost
parts of the sea;

Even there shall thy hand lead me: and thy right hand shall hold
me.

If I say, Peradventure the darkness shall cover me: then shall my
night be turned to day.

Yea, the darkness is no darkness with thee, but the night is as clear
as the day: the darkness and light to thee are both alike.

For my reins are thine: thou hast covered me in my mother's
womb.

I will give thanks unto thee, for I am fearfully and wonderfully
made: marvellous are thy works, and that my soul knoweth right
well.

My bones are not hid from thee: though I be made secretly, and
fashioned beneath in the earth.

Thine eyes did see my substance, yet being imperfect: and in thy
book were all my members written.

Which day by day were fashioned: when as yet there was none of
them.

How dear are thy counsels unto me, O God: O how great is the
sum of them!

If I tell them, they are more in number than the sand: when I wake
up I am present with thee.

Wilt thou not slay the wicked, O God: depart from me, ye blood-
thirsty men.

For they speak unrighteously against thee: and am not I grieved
with those that rise up against thee?

Yea I hate them right sore: even as though they were mine
enemies.

Try me, O God, and seek the ground of my heart: prove me, and
examine my thoughts.

Humanity

Look well if there be any way of wickedness in me: and lead me in
the way everlasting.

Psalm 139

And his gifts were that some should be apostles, some prophets,
some evangelists, some pastors and teachers, for the equipment of
the saints, for the work of ministry, for building up the body of
Christ, until we all attain to the unity of the faith and of the knowledge of the Son of God, to mature manhood, to the measure of the
stature of the fulness of Christ.

St Paul's Epistle to the Ephesians 4.11–13

Mercy: the mercy people need

Human beings need more than affection: they need mercy, from God and from one another. This section is the shortest, by no means because it is the least important, but because if mercy were all that mattered it would turn sour. To dwell for long on wrongs which need mercy is no way to forgive. Wrongs must be faced; facing them may be arduous; but the confrontation is a means to an end not an end in itself.

What people need is not even 'forgive and forget' but 'forgive and transcend'. The point of mercy, divine or human, is to be able to absorb it promptly into positive grace.

Finally, all of you, have unity of spirit, sympathy, love of the brethren, a tender heart and a humble mind. Do not return evil for evil or reviling for reviling; but on the contrary bless, for to this you have been called, that you may obtain a blessing. For 'He that would love life and see good days, let him keep his tongue from evil and his lips from speaking guile; let him turn away from evil and do right; let him seek peace, and pursue it.'

The First Epistle of St Peter 3.8–11

John said to him, 'Teacher, we saw a man casting out devils in your name, and we forbade him, because he was not following us.' But Jesus said, 'Do not forbid him; for no one who does a mighty work in my name will be able soon after to speak evil of me. For he that is not against us is for us. For truly, I say to you, whoever gives you a cup of water to drink because you bear the name of Christ, will by no means lose his reward.'

The Gospel according to St Mark 9.38–41

O Christ who holds the open gate,
O Christ who drives the furrow straight,
O Christ, the plough, O Christ, the laughter
Of holy white birds flying after,
Lo, all my heart's field red and torn,
And thou wilt bring the young green corn
The young green corn divinely springing,
The young green corn for ever singing;
And when the field is fresh and fair
Thy blessed feet shall glitter there.
And we will walk the weeded field,
And tell the golden harvest's yield,
The corn that makes the holy bread
By which the soul of man is fed,
The holy bread, the food unpriced,
Thy everlasting mercy, Christ.

John Masefield, 'The Everlasting Mercy'

Isabella: Why, all the souls that were were forfeit once;
And He that might the vantage best have took,
Found out the remedy.

William Shakespeare, *Measure for Measure*, II.2.73

But no man may deliver his brother: nor make agreement unto
  God for him;
For it cost more to redeem their souls: so that he must let that
  alone for ever.

Psalm 49.7–8

He is the image of the invisible God, the first-born of all creation; for
in him all things were created, in heaven and on earth, visible and
invisible, whether thrones or dominions or principalities or author-
ities – all things were created in him and for him. He is before all
things, and in him all things holds together. He is the head of the
body, the church; he is the beginning, the first-born from the dead,
that in everything he might be pre-eminent. For in him all the fulness of God was pleased to dwell, and through him to reconcile to
himself all things, whether on earth or in heaven, making peace by
the blood of his cross.

St Paul's Epistle to the Colossians 1.15–20

And I will give them one heart, and put a new spirit within them;
and I will take the stony heart out of their flesh, and give them a
heart of flesh, that they may walk in my statutes and keep my ordinances and obey them: and they shall be my people, and I will be
their God.

Ezekiel 11.19–20

At the round earth's imagined corners blow
Your trumpets, angels, and arise, arise
From death, you numberless infinities
Of souls, and to your scattered bodies go:
All whom the flood did, and fire shall o'er throw,
All whom war, dearth, age, agues, tyrannies,
Despair, law, chance hath slain, and you whose eyes

Shall behold God and never taste death's woe.
But let them sleep, Lord, and me mourn a space,
For if above all these my sins abound,
'Tis late to ask abundance of thy grace
When we are there. Here on this lowly ground
Teach me how to repent; for that's as good
As if thou hadst sealed my pardon with thy blood.

John Donne

Stop, Christian passer-by! – Stop, child of God,
And read with gentle breast. Beneath this sod
A poet lies, or that which once seem'd he.
O, lift one thought in prayer for S.T.C.;
That he who many a year with toil of breath
Found death in life, may here find life in death!
Mercy for praise – to be forgiven for fame
He ask'd and hoped, through Christ. Do thou the same!

Samuel Taylor Coleridge ('Epitaph')

In all time of our tribulation; in all time of our wealth; in the hour of
death, and in the day of judgement,
    Good Lord, deliver us.

The Book of Common Prayer, The Litany

He that planted the ear, shall he not hear: or he that made the eye,
    shall he not see?

Psalm 94.9

For the word of God is living and active, sharper than any two-edged
sword, piercing to the division of soul and spirit, of joints and marrow, and discerning the thoughts and intentions of the heart. And

before him no creature is hidden, but all are open and laid bare to the
eyes of him with whom we have to do.

Epistle to the Hebrews 4.12–13

Since I am coming to that Holy room
Where, with thy quire of Saints for evermore,
I shall be made thy Music; As I come
I tune the Instrument here at the door,
And what I must do then, think here before.

Whilst my Physicians by their love are grown
Cosmographers, and I their Map, who lie
Flat on this bed, that by them may be shown
That this is my South-west discovery
Per fretum febris, by these straits to die,

I joy, that in these straits, I see my West;
For, though their currents yield return to none,
What shall my West hurt me? As West and East
In all flat Maps (and I am one) are one,
So death doth touch the Resurrection.

Is the Pacific Sea my home? Or are
The Eastern riches? Is Jerusalem?
Anyan, and Magellan, and Gibraltar,
All straits, and none but straits, are ways to them,
Whether where Japhet dwelt, or Cham, or Shem.

We think that Paradise and Calvary,
Christ's Cross, and Adam's tree, stood in one place;
Look, Lord, and find both Adams met in me;
As the first Adam's sweat surrounds my face,
May the last Adam's blood my soul embrace.

Mercy

So, in his purple wrapped receive me Lord,
By these his thorns give me his other Crown;
And as to other's soul I preach'd thy word
Be this my Text, my Sermon to mine own,
Therefore, that he may raise the Lord throws down.

John Donne, 'Hymn to God my God, in my sickness'

. . . lest that by any means, when I have preached to others, I myself
should be a castaway.

St Paul's First Epistle to the Corinthians 9.27 (King James Version)

Have mercy upon me, O God, after thy great goodness: according
to the multitude of thy mercies do away mine offences.
Wash me throughly from my wickedness: and cleanse me from my
sin.
For I acknowledge my faults: and my sin is ever before me.
Against thee only have I sinned, and done this evil in thy sight: that
thou mightest be justified in thy saying, and clear when thou art
judged.
Behold, I was shapen in wickedness: and in sin hath my mother
conceived me.
But lo, thou requirest truth in the inward parts: and shalt make me
to understand wisdom secretly.
Thou shalt purge me with hyssop, and I shall be clean: thou shalt
wash me, and I shall be whiter than snow.
Thou shalt make me hear of joy and gladness: that the bones which
thou hast broken may rejoice.
Turn thy face from my sins: and blot out all my misdeeds.
Make me a clean heart, O God: and renew a right spirit within me.
Cast me not away from thy presence: and take not thy holy Spirit
from me.

O give me the comfort of thy help again: and stablish me with thy
free Spirit.

Then shall I teach thy ways unto the wicked: and sinners shall be
converted unto thee.

Deliver me from blood-guiltiness, O God, thou that art the God of
my health: and my tongue shall sing of thy righteousness.

Thou shalt open my lips, O Lord: and my mouth shall show thy
praise.

For thou desireth no sacrifice, else would I give it thee: but thou
delightest not in burnt-offerings.

The sacrifice of God is a troubled spirit: a broken and contrite
heart, O God, shalt thou not despise.

O be favourable and gracious unto Sion: build thou the walls of
Jerusalem.

Then shalt thou be pleased with the sacrifice of righteousness: then
shall they offer young bullocks upon thine altar.

Psalm 51

O Lord, one God, God the Trinity, whatsoever I have said in these
Books that comes of thy prompting, may thy people acknowledge it:
for what I have said that comes only of myself, I ask of thee and of
thy people pardon.

St Augustine, *The Trinity*, 50

Prophecy is not excluded, then, from Christian preaching; only it
must be true prophecy, a proclaiming of right, not a mere denunciation of wrong or a lament for the worthlessness of men and the evil
of society. Sometimes specific ills have to be denounced, as they
were, for instance, by Lord Shaftesbury and his friends in the struggle for the Factory Acts and the protection of children in the nine-
teenth century; or as the use of torture by Frenchmen in Algeria has
been denounced recently in France. It would seem that a Christian

embarking upon this course must first assure himself that he was fulfilling certain minimum conditions. The first, that he was certain of his facts, and as well advised as he could be in his interpretation of them. The second, that the audience addressed had some responsibility for the ills, either as people implicated in the cause of them, or as legislators capable of providing some redress, or as citizens charged with political or other influence effective enough to secure redress. The third, that the ill must be specific, and capable of being remedied. These conditions are not fulfilled in a general recital of the sins and sicknesses of society, before a congregation which, in all probability, is only in a limited and corporate sense a party to them, and with no specific action possible or invited, and no specific remedy foreseeable or foreseen. An example of this sort is the sermon which purports to be about marriage, but very soon becomes a denunciation of divorce.

G. R. Dunstan, *The Family Is Not Broken*, p. 74

They bind heavy burdens, hard to bear, and lay them on men's shoulders; but they themselves will not move them with their finger.

The Gospel according to St Matthew 23.4

Lilies that fester smell far worse than weeds.

William Shakespeare, Sonnet 94

The heart is deceitful above all things, and desperately corrupt; who can understand it?

Jeremiah 17.9

. . . Compound for sins, they are inclin'd to
By damning those they have no mind to.

Samuel Butler, *Hudibras*, I.i.213

In vain thy Reason finer webs shall draw,
Entangle Justice in her net of Law,
And right, too rigid, harden into wrong;
Still for the strong too weak, the weak too strong.

Alexander Pope, *An Essay on Man*, III, l.191

'We mustn't question the ways of Providence', said the Rector. 'Providence?' said the old woman. 'Don't yew talk to me about Providence. I've had enough o' Providence. First he took my husband, and then he took my 'taters, but there's One above as'll teach him to mend his manners, if he don't look out.'

D. L. Sayers, *The Nine Tailors*, p. 58

When God saw what they did, how they turned from their evil way, God repented of the evil which he had said he would do to them, and he did not do it.

But it displeased Jonah exceedingly and he was angry. And he prayed to the LORD and said, 'I pray thee, LORD, is not this what I said while I was yet in my country? That is why I made haste to flee to Tarshish; for I knew that thou art a gracious God and merciful, slow to anger, and abounding in steadfast love, and repentest of evil. Therefore now, O LORD, take my life from me, I beseech thee, for it is better for me to die than to live.' And the LORD said, 'Do you do well to be angry?' Then Jonah went out of the city and sat to the east of the city, and made a booth for himelf there. He sat under it in the shade, till he should see what would become of the city.

And the LORD God appointed a plant, and made it come up over Jonah, that it might be a shade over his head, to save him from his discomfort. So Jonah was exceedingly glad because of the plant. But when dawn came up the next day, God appointed a worm which attacked the plant, so that it withered. When the sun rose, God appointed a sultry east wind, and the sun beat upon the head of

Jonah so that he was faint; and he asked that he might die, and said, 'It is better for me to die than to live.' But God said to Jonah, 'Do you do well to be angry for the plant?' And he said, 'I do well to be angry, angry enough to die.' And the LORD said, 'You pity the plant, for which you did not labour, nor did you make it grow, which came into being in a night and perished in a night. And should I not pity Nineveh, that great city, in which there are more than a hundred and twenty thousand persons, who do not know their right hand from their left, and also much cattle?'

Jonah 3.10–4.11

Come, come, whoever or whatever you may be, come.
Infidel, heathen, fire-worshipper, idolater, come.
Though you have broken your penitence a hundred times,
Ours is not the temple of despair and misery, come.

Mevlana, the founder of the whirling dervishes

And hearken thou to the supplications of thy servant and of thy people Israel, when they pray toward this place; yea, hear thou in heaven thy dwelling place; and when thou hearest, forgive.

Likewise when a foreigner, who is not of thy people Israel, comes from a far country for the sake of thy great name, and thy mighty hand, and thy outstretched arm, when he comes and prays toward this house, hear thou from heaven thy dwelling place, and do according to all for which the foreigner calls to thee; in order that all the peoples of the earth may know thy name and fear thee, as do thy people Israel, and that they may know that this house which I have built is called by thy name.

2 Chronicles 6.21, 32–3 (Solomon's prayer)

Then Abraham drew near, and said, 'Wilt thou indeed destroy the righteous with the wicked? Suppose there are fifty righteous within the city; wilt thou then destroy the place and not spare it for the fifty righteous who are in it? Far be it from thee to do such a thing, to slay the righteous with the wicked, so that the righteous fare as the wicked! Far be that from thee! Shall not the Judge of all the earth do right?' And the Lord said, 'If I find at Sodom fifty righteous in the city, I will spare the whole place for their sake.'

Genesis 18.23–6

These words 'have mercy' are used in all the Christian churches and, in Orthodoxy, they are the response of the people to all the petitions suggested by the priest. Our modern translation 'have mercy' is a limited and insufficient one. The Greek word which we find in the gospel and in the early liturgies is *eleison*. *Eleison* is of the same root as *elaion*, which means the olive tree and the oil from it . . .

The oil speaks first of all of the end of the wrath of God, of the peace which God offers to the people who have offended against him; further, it speaks of God healing us in order that we should be able to live and become what we are called to be; and as he knows that we are not capable with our own strength of fulfilling either his will or the laws of our own created nature, he pours his grace abundantly on us (Rom. 5:20). He gives us power to do what we could not otherwise do.

The words *milost* and *pomiluy* in Slavonic have the same root as those which express tenderness, endearing, and when we use the words *eleison*, 'have mercy on us', *pomiluy*, we are not just asking God to save us from his wrath – we are asking for love.

Anthony Bloom, *Living Prayer*, p. 86

Mercy

A bruised reed shall he not break, and the smoking flax shall he not quench . . .

Isaiah 42.3 (Deutero-Isaiah) (King James Version)

Almighty and everlasting God, who alone workest great marvels; Send down upon our Bishops, and Curates, and all Congregations committed to their charge, the healthful Spirit of thy grace; and that they may truly please thee, pour upon them the continual dew of thy blessing. Grant this, O Lord, for the honour of our Advocate and Mediator, Jesus Christ. *Amen*

The Book of Common Prayer, A prayer for the clergy and people

Yet you must arm yourself with Expectations of their Infirmities, and resolv nobly to forgive them: not in a sordid and Cowardly maner, by taking no notice of them: nor in a Dim or Lazy maner, by letting them alone: but in a Divine and Illustrious maner by chiding them meekly, and vigourously rendering and showering down all kinds of Benefits.

Thomas Traherne, *Centuries*, I.84

Sir Robert Chiltern: Why can't you women love us, faults and all? Why do you place us on monstrous pedestals? We have all feet of clay, women as well as men; but when we men love women, we love them knowing their weaknesses, their follies, their imperfections, love them all the more, it may be, for that reason. It is not the perfect, but the imperfect, who have need of love. It is when we are wounded by our own hands, or by the hands of others, that love should come to cure us – else what use is love at all?

Oscar Wilde, *An Ideal Husband*, II

Be merciful, even as your Father is merciful. Judge not, and you will not be judged: condemn not, and you will not be condemned: forgive, and you shall be forgiven: give, and it will be given to you; good measure, pressed down, shaken together, running over, will be put into your lap. For the measure you give will be the measure you get back.

Luke 6.36

Polonius: My lord, I will use them according to their desert.
Hamlet: God's bodikins, man, much better; use every man after his desert, and who should 'scape whipping? Use them after your own honour and dignity: the less they deserve, the more merit is in your bounty.

William Shakespeare, *Hamlet*, II.2

A little kindness – and putting her hair in papers – would do wonders with her –

Lewis Carroll, *Through the Looking Glass*, Chapter 9

'They have both', said she, 'been deceived, I dare say, in some way or other, of which we can form no idea. Interested people have perhaps misrepresented each to the other. It is, in short, impossible for us to conjecture the causes or circumstances which may have alienated them, without actual blame on either side.'

'Very true, indeed; and now, my dear Jane, what have you got to say in behalf of the interested people who have probably been concerned in the business? Do clear *them*, too, or we shall be obliged to think ill of somebody.'

Jane Austen, *Pride and Prejudice*, Chapter 17

Admonish a friend, it may be he hath not done it: and if he have
 done it, that he do it no more.
Admonish thy friend, it may be he hath not said it: and if he have,
 that he speak it not again.
Admonish a friend: for many times it is a slander, and believe not
 every tale.
There is one that slippeth in his speech, but not from his heart; and
 who is he that hath not offended with his tongue?
Admonish thy neighbour before thou threaten him; and not being
 angry, give place to the law of the most High.

Ecclesiasticus 19.13 (King James Version)

He that answereth a matter before he heareth it, it is folly and shame
unto him.

Proverbs 18.12 (King James Version)

. . . but whoever shall say, Thou fool, shall be in danger of hell fire.

The Gospel according to St Matthew 5.22 (King James Version)

'Bobby won't enjoy himself much, and he won't race much either',
said Nicholas with a grim chuckle; 'his boots are hurting him.
They're too tight.'

'Why didn't he tell me they were hurting?' asked the aunt with
some asperity.

'He told you twice, but you weren't listening. You often don't listen when we tell you important things.'

Saki, 'The Lumber Room'

Macbeth: . . . and under him
　　　　My genius is rebuk'd, as it is said
　　　　Mark Antony's was by Caesar.

William Shakespeare, Macbeth, III.1

Tread softly because you tread on my dreams.

W. B. Yeats, 'Aedh wishes for the cloths of heaven'

Whate'er my sins might be, *thou* wert not sent
To be the Nemesis that should requite –
Nor did Heaven choose so near an instrument.

Lord Byron, 'Lines on hearing that Lady Byron was ill'

. . . but for our ceaseless labour . . . the variety of usage within the
Church of England might have become a perfect hotbed of charity
and humility.

C. S. Lewis, The Screwtape Letters, 16

Keep, we beseech thee, O Lord, thy Church with thy perpetual
mercy: and, because the frailty of man without thee cannot but fall,
keep us ever by thy help from all things hurtful, and lead us to all
things profitable to our salvation; through Jesus Christ our Lord.
Amen.

The Book of Common Prayer, Collect for the Fifteenth Sunday after Trinity

With what shall I come before the LORD, and bow myself before
God on high? Shall I come before him with burnt offerings, with
calves a year old? Will the LORD be pleased with thousands of rams,
with ten thousands of rivers of oil? Shall I give my first-born for my
transgression, the fruit of my body for the sin of my soul? He has
showed you, O man, what is good; and what does the LORD require

of you, but to do justice, and to love kindness, and to walk humbly
with your God?

Micah 6.6

But Naaman was angry, and went away, saying . . . 'Are not Abana
and Pharpar, the rivers of Damascus, better than all the waters of
Israel? Could I not wash in them and be clean?' So he turned and
went away in a rage. But his servants came near and said to him, 'My
father, if the prophet had commanded you to do some great thing,
would you not have done it? How much rather then, when he says to
you, "Wash, and be clean?"' So he went down and dipped himself
seven times in Jordan, according to the word of the man of God; and
his flesh was restored like the flesh of a little child, and he was clean.

2 Kings 5.11–13

Sweetest Saviour, if my soul
Were but worth the having,
Quickly should I then controll
Any thought of waving.
But when all my care and pains
Cannot give the name of gains
To thy wretch so full of stains,
What delight or hope remains?

What, Child, is the ballance thine,
Thine the poise and measure?
If I say, Thou shalt be mine;
Finger not my treasure.
What the gains in having thee
Do amount to, onely he,
Who for man was sold, can see;
That transferr'd th' accounts to me.

But as I can see no merit,
Leading to this favour:
So the way to fit me for it
Is beyond my savour.
As the reason then is thine;
So the way is none of mine:
I disclaim the whole designe:
Sinne disclaims and I resigne.

That is all, if that I could
Get without repining;
And my clay, my creature, would
Follow my resigning:
That as I did freely part
With my glorie and desert,
Left all joyes to feel all smart –
Ah! no more: thou break'st my heart.

George Herbert, 'Dialogue'

Then he showed me the river of the water of life, bright as crystal,
flowing from the throne of God and of the Lamb through the middle
of the street of the city; also, on either side of the river, the tree of life
with its twelve kinds of fruit, yielding its fruit each month; and the
leaves of the tree were for the healing of the nations.

Revelation 22.1–2

Be mindful, O Lord, of thy people present here before thee, and of
those who are absent through age, sickness or infirmity. Care for the
infants, guide the young, support the aged, encourage the faint-
hearted, collect the scattered, and bring the wandering to thy fold.
Travel with the voyagers, defend the widows, shield the orphans,
deliver the captives, heal the sick. Succour all who are in tribulation,

necessity or distress. Remember for good all those that love us, and those that hate us; and those who have desired us, unworthy as we are, to pray for them. And those whom we have forgotten, do thou, O Lord, remember. For thou art the Helper of the helpless, the Saviour of the lost, the Refuge of the wanderer, the Healer of the sick. Thou, who knowest each man's need, and hast heard his prayer, grant unto each according to thy merciful loving kindness and thy eternal love; through Jesus Christ our Lord. Amen.

A prayer of the Eastern Church, from Frank Colquhoun, *Parish Prayers*

. . . even to your old age I am He, and to grey hairs I will carry you. I have made, and I will bear; I will carry and will save.

Isaiah 46.4 (Deutero-Isaiah)

Thou, O God, art praised in Zion: and unto thee shall the vow be
    performed in Jerusalem.
Thou that hearest the prayer: unto thee shall all flesh come.
My misdeeds prevail against me: O be thou merciful unto our sins.
Blessed is the man, whom thou choosest, and receivest unto thee:
    he shall dwell in thy court, and shall be satisfied with the
    pleasures of thy house, even of thy holy temple.
Thou shalt show us wonderful things in thy righteousness, O God
    of our salvation: thou that art the hope of all the ends of the
    earth, and of them that remain in the broad sea.
Who in his strength setteth fast the mountains, and is girded about
    with power.
Who stilleth the raging of the sea: and the noise of his waves, and
    the madness of the people.
They also that dwell in the uttermost parts of the earth shall be
    afraid at thy tokens: thou that makest the outgoings of the
    morning and evening to praise thee.

Thou visitest the earth, and blessest it: thou makest it very
    plenteous.
The river of God is full of water: thou preparest her corn, for so
    thou providest for the earth.
Thou waterest her furrows, thou sendest rain into the little valleys
    thereof: thou makest it soft with the drops of rain, and blessest
    the increase of it.
Thou crownest the year with thy goodness: thy clouds drop fatness.
They shall drop upon the dwellings of the wilderness: and the little
    hills shall rejoice on every side.
The folds shall be full of sheep: the valleys also shall stand so thick
    with corn, that they shall laugh and sing.

Psalm 65

O God of unchangeable power and eternal light, look favourably on
thy whole church, that wonderful and sacred mystery; and, by the
tranquil operation of thy perpetual providence, carry out the work of
man's salvation; and let the whole world feel and see that things
which were cast down are being raised up, that those things which
had grown old are being made new, and that all things are returning
to perfection, through him from whom they took their origin, even
through our Lord Jesus Christ.

Gelasian Sacramentary

Grace: the grace people receive

This longest and central section starts with God's grace, as some human beings have discerned it and responded to it. It moves to human grace and back to God's grace again.

Speaking of human grace is not paradoxical nor presumptuous. We do not call the moon dark because its light is reflected from the sun. To think of human creatures as essentially graceless would be no honour to their Creator. Human grace is a matter of loving and liking, affirming not denying. If God minds about people, people may and should mind about one another and about themselves. Not to mind is literally hellish.

When hell is defeated, it is overcome by blessing; and there is human blessing as well as divine. Human beings are able to be grace-givers, not confined to a passive role. They can indeed do things for one another. Better still, they can co-operate with one another. They have scope for variegated vocations, particular callings and special affections. Enjoying one another's company is a primary human grace. Parents and children, friends, husbands and wives are good to each other in ways which make talk about duty simply inadequate.

All this can be told in secular terms. What Christian belief adds is that human grace is founded on divine grace. The centre of Christian faith is one historical human being who embodied the grace of God on earth.

His followers keep in touch with him still by eating and drinking together in his name. The familiar human grace of a shared meal becomes a sacrament, an outward and visible sign of the grace of God. One of the names of this means of grace is the Eucharist, the Thanksgiving. Christians asking how they can find grace can understand that grace and gratitude *are linked in their basic meaning, not just in the common origin of the words. To set about following is the best way of finding.*

◈

I will lift up mine eyes unto the hills: from whence cometh my help.
My help cometh even from the Lord: who hath made heaven and
    earth.
He will not suffer thy foot to be moved: and he that keepeth thee will
    not sleep.
Behold, he that keepeth Israel: shall neither slumber nor sleep.
The Lord himself is thy keeper: the Lord is thy defence upon thy
    right hand;
So that the sun shall not burn thee by day: neither the moon by
    night.
The Lord shall preserve thee from all evil: yea, it is even he that shall
    keep thy soul.
The Lord shall preserve thy going out, and thy coming in: from this
    time forth for evermore.

Psalm 121

I was glad when they said unto me: We will go into the house of the
    Lord.

Psalm 122.1

O praise the Lord with me: and let us magnify his Name together.

Psalm 34.3

The antidote to sin is not duty but praise.

David Jenkins, *What Is Man?*, p. 121

To pray is to descend with mind into the heart and there to stand, in silence and stillness, before the face of the Lord, ever present, all-seeing, within you.

Sentence used by Lakshman Wickremesinghe

For this commandment which I command you this day is not too hard for you, neither is it far off. It is not in heaven, that you should say, 'Who will go up for us to heaven, and bring it to us, that we may hear it and do it?' Neither is it beyond the sea, that you should say, 'Who will go over the sea for us, and bring it to us, that we may hear it, and do it?' But the word is very near you; it is in your mouth and in your heart, so that you can do it.

Deuteronomy 30.11–14

Raise the stone, and there thou shalt find me, cleave the wood and there am I.

Oxyrhynchus Papyri

Likewise the Spirit helps us in our weakness; for we do not know how to pray as we ought, but the Spirit himself intercedes for us with sighs too deep for words.

St Paul's Epistle to the Romans 8.26

For the closed heart does not bar thy sight into it, nor does the hardness of our heart hold back thy hands.

St Augustine, *Confessions*, V.1

. . . but they who wait for the LORD shall renew their strength, they shall mount up with wings like eagles, they shall run and not be weary, they shall walk, and not faint.

Isaiah 40.31 (Deutero-Isaiah)

All of you be subject one to another, and be clothed with humility: for God resisteth the proud, and giveth grace to the humble. Humble yourselves, therefore, under the mighty hand of God, that he may exalt you in due time; Casting all your care upon him, for he careth for you. Be sober, be vigilant; because your adversary the devil, as a roaring lion, walketh about seeking whom he may devour: whom resist, steadfast in the faith, knowing that the same afflictions are accomplished in your brethren that are in the world. But the God of all grace, who hath called us into his eternal glory by Christ Jesus, after that ye have suffered a while, make you perfect, stablish, strengthen, settle you. To him be glory and dominion for ever and ever. Amen.

The First Epistle of St Peter 5.5–11 (King James Version)

Forth in thy name, O Lord, I go,
My daily labour to pursue;
Thee, only thee, resolved to know,
In all I think, or speak, or do.

The task thy wisdom hath assigned
O let me cheerfully fulfil;
In all my works thy presence find,
And prove thine acceptable will.

Preserve me from my calling's snare,
And hide my simple heart above,
Above the thorns of choking care,
The gilded baits of worldly love.

[118]

Thee may I set at thy right hand,
Whose eyes my inmost substance see,
And labour on at thy command,
And offer all my works to thee.

Give me to bear thy easy yoke,
And every moment watch and pray,
And still to things eternal look,
And hasten to thy glorious day.

For thee delightfully employ
Whate'er thy bounteous grace hath given,
And run my course with even joy,
And closely walk with thee to heaven.

Charles Wesley

Rejoice in the Lord alway: and again I say, Rejoice. Let your modera-
tion be known unto all men. The Lord is at hand. Be careful for nothing; but in every thing by prayer and supplication with thanksgiving
let your requests be made known unto God. And the peace of God,
which passeth all understanding, shall keep your hearts and minds
through Christ Jesus. Finally, brethren, whatsoever things are true,
whatsoever things are honest, whatsoever things are just, whatsoever things are pure, whatsoever things are lovely, whatsoever
things are of good report; if there be any virtue, and if there be any
praise, think on these things.

St Paul's Epistle to the Philippians 4.4–8 (King James Version)

Fret not thyself because of the ungodly.

Psalm 37.1

xv   From being anxious, or secure,
Dead clods of sadness, or light squibs of mirth,
From thinking that great courts immure
All, or no happiness, or that this earth
Is only for our prison framed,
Or that thou art covetous
To them whom thou lov'st, or that they are maimed
From reaching this world's sweet, who seek thee thus
With all their might, good Lord, deliver us.

xvi   From needing danger to be good,
From owing thee yesterday's tears today,
From trusting so much to thy blood
That in that hope we wound our souls away,
From bribing thee with alms to excuse
Some sin more burdenous,
From light affecting, in religion, news,
From thinking us all soul, neglecting thus
Our mutual duties, Lord, deliver us.

xvii   From tempting Satan to tempt us
By our connivance or slack company,
From measuring ill by vicious,
Neglecting to choke sin's spawn, vanity,
From indiscreet humility,
Which might be scandalous
And cast reproach on Christianity,
From being spies, or to spies pervious,
From thirst, or scorn of fame, deliver us.

xxi   When senses, which thy soldiers are,
We arm against thee, and they fight for sin,
When want, sent but to tame, doth war
And work despair a breach to enter in,

Grace

When plenty, God's image and seal,
Makes us idolatrous,
And love it, not him, whom it should reveal,
When we are moved to seem religious
Only to vent wit, Lord deliver us.

John Donne, The Litanie

Christians spend their time interceding, and at times I listen to these intercessions with fear because to me intercession means an involvement that may spell death; and I am frightened when I hear a congregation of people intercede for one need after another, piling up on their shoulders all the needs of the world just for the time Evensong lasts. After that they put it down on God's shoulders, and they go out elevated with a new emotion.

Anthony Bloom, God and Man, p. 43

'Poor Becky, poor Becky!' said Emmy. 'How thankful, how thankful I ought to be' (though I doubt whether that practice of piety inculcated upon us by our womankind in early youth, namely, to be thankful because we are better off than somebody else, be a very rational religious exercise).

William Makepeace Thackeray, Vanity Fair, Chapter 66

Later on you can venture on what may be called the Generous Conflict Illusion. This game is best played with more than two players, in a family with grown-up children for example. Something quite trivial, like having tea in the garden, is proposed. One member takes care to make it quite clear (though not in so many words) that he would rather not but is, of course, prepared to do so out of 'Unselfishness'. The others instantly withdraw their proposal, ostensibly through their 'Unselfishness', but really because they don't want to be used as a sort of lay figure on which the first speaker practises petty altruisms. But he is not going to be done out of his debauch of Unselfishness either. He insists on doing 'what the others want'. They insist on doing what he wants. Passions are roused. Soon someone is saying 'Very well then, I won't have any tea at all!' and a real quarrel ensues with bitter resentment on both sides. You see how it is done? If each side had been frankly contending for its own real wish, they would all have kept within the bounds of reason and courtesy; but just because the contention is reversed and each side is fighting the other side's battle, all the bitterness which really flows from thwarted self-righteousness and obstinacy and the accumulated grudges of the last ten years is concealed from them by the nominal or official 'Unselfishness' of what they are doing or, at least, held to be excused by it.

C. S. Lewis, *The Screwtape Letters*, 26

A shrimp who sought his lady shrimp
Could catch no glimpse
Not even a glimp.
At times, translucence
Is rather a nuisance.

Ogden Nash, 'Fellow Creatures: The Shrimp'

Don Pedro: . . . out of question, you were born in a merry hour.
Beatrice: No, sure, my lord, my mother cried; but then there was a star danced, and under that was I born.

William Shakespeare, *Much Ado About Nothing*, II.I

'If it was not for the entail, I should not mind it.'
'What should you not mind?'
'I should not mind anything at all.'

Grace

'Let us be thankful that you are preserved from a state of such insen-
sibility.'

Jane Austen, *Pride and Prejudice*, Chapter 23

More than we wished we knew the blessing then
Of vigorous hunger.

William Wordsworth, *The Prelude*, II

Packed in my skin from head to toe
Is one I know and do not know . . .

His name's Indifference.
Nothing offending he is all offence;
Can stare at beauty's bosom coldly
And at Christ's crucifixion boldly;
Can note with a lack-lustre eye
Victim and murderer go by;
Can pore upon the maze of lust
And watch the lecher fall to dust
With the same glance; content can wait
By a green bank at Eden's gate
To see the first blood flow and see nought then
Except a bright and glittering rain.
If I could drive this demon out
I'd put all time's display to rout.
Its wounds would turn to flowers and nothing be
But the first Garden. The one tree
Would stand for ever safe and fair
And Adam's hand stop in the air.
Or so I dream when at my door
I hear my Soul, my visitor.

Edwin Muir, *Variations on a Time Theme* IX

But flippancy is the best of all. In the first place it is very economical. Only a clever human can make a real Joke about virtue, or indeed anything else; any of them can be trained to talk *as if* virtue were funny. Among flippant people the Joke is always assumed to have been made. No one actually makes it; but every serious subject is discussed in a manner which implies that they have already found a ridiculous side to it. If prolonged, the habit of Flippancy builds up around a man the finest armour-plating against the Enemy that I know, and it is quite free from the dangers inherent in the other sources of laughter. It is a thousand miles away from joy: it deadens, instead of sharpening, the intellect; and it excites no affection between those who practise it.

C. S. Lewis, *The Screwtape Letters*, 11

Faustus: Where are you damned?
Mephistopheles: In hell.
Faustus: How comes it then that thou art out of hell?
Mephistopheles: Why this is hell, nor am I out of it.

Christopher Marlowe, *Doctor Faustus*, II.3

l. 123   The very deep did rot: O Christ!
       That ever this should be!
       Yea, slimy things did crawl with legs
       Upon the slimy sea . . .

l. 232   Alone, alone, all, all alone,
       Alone on a wide wide sea!
       And never a saint took pity on
       My soul in agony.

       The many men, so beautiful!
       And they all dead did lie:
       And a thousand thousand slimy things
       Lived on; and so did I.

I looked upon the rotting sea,
And drew my eyes away;
I looked upon the rotting deck,
And there the dead men lay.

I looked to heaven, and tried to pray;
But or ever a prayer had gusht,
A wicked whisper came, and made
My heart as dry as dust.

I closed my lids, and kept them close,
And the balls like pulses beat;
For the sky and the sea, and the sea and the sky
Lay like a load on my weary eye,
And the dead were at my feet.

The cold sweat melted from their limbs,
Nor rot nor reek did they:
The look wherewith they looked on me
Had never passed away.

An orphan's curse would drag to hell
A spirit from on high;
But oh! more horrible than that
Is the curse in a dead man's eye!
Seven days, seven nights, I saw that curse,
And yet I could not die.

The moving Moon went up the sky,
And no where did abide:
Softly she was going up,
And a star or two beside –
Her beams bemocked the sultry main,
Like April hoar-frost spread;

But where the ship's huge shadow lay,
The charméd water burnt alway
A still and awful red.

Beyond the shadow of the ship,
I watched the water-snakes:
They moved in tracks of shining white,
And where they reared, the elfish light
Fell off in hoary flakes.

Within the shadow of the ship
I watched their rich attire:
Blue, glossy green, and velvet black,
They coiled and swam; and every track
Was a flash of golden fire.

O happy living things! no tongue
Their beauty might declare:
A spring of love gushed from my heart,
And I blessed them unaware:
Sure my kind saint took pity on me,
And I blessed them unaware.

That self-same moment I could pray;
And from my neck so free
The albatross fell off, and sank
Like lead into the sea.

Samuel Taylor Coleridge, 'The Rime of the Ancient Mariner'

The Corn was Orient and Immortal Wheat, which never should be reaped, nor was ever sown. I thought it had stood from everlasting to everlasting. The Dust and Stones of the Street were as Precious as GOLD. The Gates were at first the End of the World. The Green

Grace

Trees when I saw them first through one of the Gates Transported and Ravished me; their Sweetnes and unusual Beauty made my Heart leap, and almost mad with Extasie, they were such strange and Wonderfull Things: The Men! O what Venerable and Reverend Creatures did the Aged seem! Immortal Cherubims! And young Men glittering and Sparkling Angels and Maids strange Seraphick Pieces of Life and Beauty! Boys and Girles Tumbling in the Street, and Playing, were moving Jewels. I knew not that they were Born or should Die. But all things abided Eternaly as they were in their Proper Places. Eternity was Manifest in the Light of the Day, and som thing infinit Behind evry thing appeared: which talked with my Expectation and moved my Desire. The Citie seemed to stand in Eden, or to be Built in Heaven. The Streets were mine, the Temple was mine, the People were mine, their Cloths and Gold and Silver was mine, as much as their Sparkling Eys, Fair Skins and ruddy faces. The Skies were mine, and so were the Sun and Moon and Stars, and all the World was mine, and I the only Spectator and Enjoyer of it.

Thomas Traherne, *Centuries*, III.3

He that can apprehend and consider vice with all her baits and seeming pleasures, and yet abstain, and yet distinguish, and yet prefer that which is truly better, he is the true wayfaring Christian. I cannot praise a fugitive and cloistered virtue, unexercised and unbreathed, that never sallies out and sees her adversary, but slinks out of the race, where that immortal garland is to be run for, not without dust and heat.

John Milton, *Areopagitica*

Whatever your hand finds to do, do it with your might . . .

Ecclesiastes 9.10

They also shall bring forth more fruit in their age: and shall be fat
and well-liking.

Psalm 92.13

Know what is the principal service that you are called to, and avoid
avocations: especially magistrates and ministers, and those that
have great and public work, must here take heed. For if you be not
very wise and watchful, the tempter will draw you, before you are
aware, into such a multitude of diverting care or business, that shall
seem to be your duties, as shall make you almost unprofitable in the
world.

Richard Baxter, 'The Christian Directory', in Beach and Niebuhr (eds), Christian
Ethics: Sources of the Living Tradition, pp. 313–14

That is very important: one of the things which we must unlearn, is
looking at the clock. If you are walking somewhere and are aware
that you are late, you look at your watch. But you cannot walk as
quickly while you look at your wrist as if you simply look straight
ahead. And whether you are aware that it is seven minutes or five or
three minutes, you are none the less late. So add a starting time and
you will be there on time, or else if you are late, walk as fast and as
briskly as you can. When you are at the door, have a look to see how
contrite you must look when the door is opened!

Anthony Bloom, School for Prayer, p. 55

On one occasion Coleridge was holding forth on the effects produced by his preaching, and appealed to Lamb, 'You have heard me
preach, I think?' 'I have never heard you do anything else,' was the
reply.

Caroline Fox, Memories of old friends (1872)

Grace

Obsairve! Per annum we'll have here two thousand souls
    aboard –
Think not I dare to justify myself before the Lord,
But – average fifteen hunder souls safe-borne fra' port to port –
I *am* of service to my kind. Ye wadna blame the thought?

Rudyard Kipling, 'McAndrew's Hymn'

Shew thy servants thy work: and their children thy glory.
And the glorious Majesty of the Lord our God be upon us: prosper
    thou the work of our hands upon us, O prosper thou our handy-
    work.

Psalm 90.16–17

Stir up, we beseech thee, O Lord, the wills of thy faithful people; that
they, plenteously bringing forth the fruit of good works, may of thee
be plenteously rewarded.

The Book of Common Prayer, Collect for the Sunday before Advent

But the fruit of the Sprit is love, joy, peace, patience, kindness, goodness, faithfulness, gentleness, self-control; against such there is no
law.

St Paul's Epistle to the Galatians 5.22–3

And he shall be like a tree planted by the waterside: that will bring
    forth his fruit in due season.

Psalm 1.3

I appeal to you therefore, brethren, by the mercies of God, to present
your bodies as a living sacrifice, holy and acceptable to God, which is
your spiritual worship. Do not be conformed to this world but be

transformed by the renewal of your mind, that you may prove what is the will of God, what is good and acceptable and perfect.

For by the grace given to me I bid every one among you not to think of himself more highly than he ought to think, but to think with sober judgment, each according to the measure of faith which God has assigned him. For as in one body we have many members, and all the members do not have the same function, so we, though many, are one body in Christ, and individually members one of another. Having gifts that differ according to the grace given to us, let us use them: if prophecy, in proportion to our faith; if service, in our serving; he who teaches, in his teaching; he who exhorts, in his exhortation; he who contributes, in liberality; he who gives aid, with zeal; he who does acts of mercy, with cheerfulness.

Let love be genuine; hate what is evil; hold fast to what is good; love one another with brotherly affection; outdo one another in showing honour. Never flag in zeal, be aglow with the Spirit, serve the Lord. Rejoice in your hope, be patient in tribulation, be constant in prayer. Contribute to the needs of the saints, practise hospitality.

Bless those who persecute you: bless, and do not curse them. Rejoice with those who rejoice, weep with those who weep. Live in harmony with one another; do not be haughty, but associate with the lowly. Never be conceited. Repay no one evil for evil, but take thought for what is noble in the sight of all. If possible, so far as it depends upon you, live peaceably with all. Beloved, never avenge yourselves, but leave it to the wrath of God: for it is written, 'Vengeance is mine; I will repay, says the Lord.' No, 'if your enemy is hungry, feed him; if he is thirsty, give him drink: for by so doing you will heap burning coals upon his head.' Do not be overcome by evil, but overcome evil with good.

St Paul's Epistle to the Romans 12

Grace

This ae nighte, this ae nighte,
– *Every nighte and alle,*
Fire and fleet and candle-lighte,
And Christe receive thy saule.

When thou from hence away art past,
– *Every nighte and alle,*
To Whinny-muir thou com'st at last;
And Christe receive thy saule.

If ever thou gavest hosen and shoon,
– *Every nighte and alle,*
Sit thee doun and put them on;
And Christe receive thy saule.

If hosen and shoon thou ne'er gav'st nane
– *Every nighte and alle,*
The whinnes sall prick thee to the bare bane;
And Christe receive thy saule.

From Whinny-muir when thou may'st pass,
– *Every nighte and alle,*
To Brig O' Dread thou com'st at last
And Christe receive they saule.

From Brig O' Dread when thou may'st pass,
– *Every night and alle,*
To Purgatory fire thou com'st at last;
And Christe receive thy saule.

If ever thou gavest meat or drink,
– *Every nighte and alle,*
The fire sall never make thee shrink;
And Christe receive thy saule.

If meat or drink thou ne'er gav'st nane,
– *Every nighte and alle,*
The fire will burn thee to the bare bane;
And Christe receive thy saule.

This ae nighte, this ae nighte,
– *Every nighte and alle,*
Fire and fleet and candle-lighte,
And Christe receive thy saule.

Anonymous, 'A Lyke-Wake Dirge'

Is this a Fast, to keep
   The larder lean
     And clean
From fat of veals and sheep?

Is it to quit the dish
   Of flesh, yet still
     To fill
The platter high with fish?

Is it to fast an hour
   Or ragg'd to go
     Or show
A down-cast look and sour?

No: 'tis a Fast to dole
   Thy sheaf of wheat
     And meat
Unto the hungry soul.

It is to fast from strife
   And old debate
     And hate;
To circumcise thy life.

To show a heart grief-rent;
   To starve thy sin,
     Not bin;
And that's to keep thy Lent.

Robert Herrick, 'To keep a true Lent'

'None can usurp this height', returned that shade,
'But those to whom the miseries of this world
Are misery, and will not let them rest.'

John Keats, *The Fall of Hyperion: A Dream* I

When God removes evils in the human sort of way, it is commonly by the employment of human hands.

Austin Farrer, *Saving Belief*, p. 57

Portia: That light we see is burning in my hall.
         How far that little candle throws his beams!
         So shines a good deed in a naughty world.

William Shakespeare, *The Merchant of Venice*, V.1

Then the righteous will answer him, 'Lord, when did we see thee hungry and feed thee, or thirsty and give thee drink? And when did we see thee a stranger and welcome thee, or naked and clothe thee? And when did we see thee sick or in prison and visit thee?' And the King will answer them, 'Truly, I say to you, as you did it to one of the least of these my brethren, you did it to me.'

The Gospel according to St Matthew 25.37–40

My weight is my love . . .

St Augustine, *Confessions*, XIII.9

There are who ask not if thine eye
Be on them; who, in love and truth,
Where no misgiving is, rely
Upon the genial sense of youth;
Glad Hearts! without reproach or blot;
Who do thy work, and know it not:
Oh! if through confidence misplaced
They fail, thy saving arms, dread Power! around them cast.

William Wordsworth, 'Ode to Duty'

Whoso dwelleth under the defence of the most High: shall abide
under the shadow of the Almighty.

I will say unto the Lord, Thou art my hope, and my strong hold: my
God, in him will I trust.

For he shall deliver thee from the snare of the hunter: and from the
noisome pestilence.

He shall defend thee under his wings, and thou shalt be safe under
his feathers: his faithfulness and truth shall be thy shield and
buckler.

Thou shalt not be afraid for any terror by night: nor for the arrow
that flieth by day;

For the pestilence that walketh in darkness: nor for the sickness
that destroyeth in the noon-day.

A thousand shall fall beside thee, and ten thousand at thy right
hand: but it shall not come nigh thee.

Yea, with thine eyes shalt thou behold: and see the reward of the
ungodly.

For thou, Lord, art my hope: thou hast set thine house of defence
very high.

There shall no evil happen unto thee: neither shall any plague
come nigh thy dwelling.

For he shall give his angels charge over thee: to keep thee in all thy
ways.

They shall bear thee in their hands: that thou hurt not thy foot
    against a stone.
Thou shalt go upon the lion and the adder: the young lion and the
    dragon shalt thou tread under thy feet.
Because he hath set his love upon me, therefore will I deliver him: I
    will set him up, because he hath known my Name.
He shall call upon me, and I will hear him: yea, I am with him in
    trouble; I will deliver him, and bring him to honour.
With long life will I satisfy him: and shew him my salvation.

Psalm 91

On parent knees, a naked new-born child,
Weeping thou sat'st while all around thee smiled:
So live, that sinking to thy life's last sleep,
Calm thou may'st smile, whilst all around thee weep.

William Jones, 'Epigram'

Lord, who shall dwell in thy tabernacle: or who shall rest upon thy
    holy hill?
Even he, that leadeth an uncorrupt life: and doeth the thing that is
    right, and speaketh the truth from his heart.
He that hath used no deceit in his tongue, nor done evil to his
    neighbour: and hath not slandered his neighbour.
He that setteth not by himself, but is lowly in his own eyes: and
    maketh much of them that fear the Lord.
He that sweareth unto his neighbour, and disappointeth him not:
    though it were to his own hindrance.
He that hath not given his money upon usury: nor taken reward
    against the innocent.
Whoso doeth these things: shall never die.

Psalm 15

To the memory of George Lavington DD
Who having early distinguished himself
By a conscientious and disinterested attachment
To the cause of Liberty and the Reformation
Was successively advanced to dignities
In the Cathedrals of Worcester and St. Paul's
And lastly to the episcopal chair of this Church.

Endowed by Nature with superior Abilities
Rich in a great variety of acquired knowledge
In the study of the holy Scriptures consummate
He never ceased to improve his Talents
Nor to employ them to the noblest Purposes.
An instructive animated and convincing Preacher
A determined Enemy to Idolatry and Persecution
A successful Exposer of Pretence and Enthusiasm.

Happy in his services to the Church of Christ
Happier, who could unite such extensive cares
With a strict attention to his immediate charge!
His absences from his Diocese were short and rare;
And his Presence was endeared to his Clergy
By an easy access and a graceful Hospitality,
A winning conversation and a condescending Deportment.
Unaffected Sanctity dignified his Instructions,
And indulgent Candor sweet'ned his Government.

At length having eminently discharged the Duties
Of a Man a Christian and a Prelate
Prepared by habitual Meditation
To resign Life without Regret
To meet Death without Tears
He expired with the Praises of God upon his lips
In his 79th Year September 13th 1762.

Epitaph in Exeter Cathedral

And, that there may never be wanting a succession of persons duly qualified for the service of God in church and state, ye shall implore his blessing on all places of religious and useful learning, particularly on our Universities.

From The bidding prayer of the University of Oxford

St Paul says and I do in part agree.

Claude Jenkins, Sermon at Christ Church, Oxford (remembered)

And if the subject be curious and interesting, the book carries us, in a manner, into company; and unites the two greatest and purest pleasures of human life, study and society.

David Hume, *Dialogues concerning Natural Religion*, Introduction

Honour a physician with the honour due unto him for the uses
  which ye may have of him: for the Lord hath created him.
For of the most High cometh healing; and he shall receive honour
  of the King.
The skill of the physician shall lift up his head: and in the sight of
  great men he shall be in admiration.
The Lord hath created medicines out of the earth; and he that is
  wise will not abhor them.
Was not the water made sweet with wood, that the virtue thereof
  might be known?
And he hath given men skill, that he might be honoured in his
  marvellous works.
With such doth he heal men, and taketh away their pains.
Of such doth the apothecary make a confection; and of his works
  there is no end; and from him is peace over all the earth.
My son, in thy sickness be not negligent: but pray unto the Lord,
  and he will make thee whole.

Leave off from sin, and order thine hands aright, and cleanse thy
heart from all wickedness.

Give a sweet savour, and a memorial of fine flour; and make a fat
offering, as not being.

Then give place to the physician, for the Lord hath created him: let
him not go from thee, for thou hast need of him.

There is a time when in their hands there is good success.

For they shall also pray unto the Lord, that he would prosper that,
which they give for ease and remedy to prolong life.

Ecclesiasticus 38.1–14 (King James Version)

He maketh the barren woman to keep house: and to be a joyful
mother of children.

Psalm 113.8

That our sons shall grow up as the young plants: and that our
daughters may be as the polished corners of the temple.

Psalm 144.12

Put thou thy trust in the Lord, and be doing good: dwell in the land,
and verily thou shalt be fed.

Delight thou in the Lord: and he shall give thee thy heart's desire.

Psalm 37.3–4

O stablish me according to thy word, that I may live: and let me not
be disappointed of my hope.

Hold thou me up and then I shall be safe: yea, my delight shall be
ever in thy statutes.

Psalm 119.116–17

Grace

Every good gift, and every perfect gift is from above, and cometh down from the Father of lights, with whom there is no variableness, neither shadow of turning. Of his own will begat he us with the Word of truth, that we should be a kind of first-fruits of his creatures. Wherefore, my beloved brethren, let every man be swift to hear, slow to speak, slow to wrath; for the wrath of man worketh not the righteousness of God. Wherefore lay apart all filthiness and superfluity of naughtiness, and receive with meekness the engrafted Word, which is able to save your souls.

The Epistle of St James 1.17–21 (King James Version)

I was angry with my friend:
I told my wrath, my wrath did end.
I was angry with my foe:
I told it not, my wrath did grow.

William Blake, 'A poison tree'

Men are not to be loved as things to be consumed, but in the manner of friendship and goodwill leading us to do things for the benefit of those we love. And if there is nothing we can do, goodwill alone is enough for the lover. We should not want there to be unfortunates, so that we may exercise works of mercy. You give bread to the hungry; but it would be better that no one should hunger, and that you should not have to give. You clothe the naked; would that all were so clothed that there were no need for it! You bury the dead: but we long for that life in which there is no dying. You reconcile men at law with one another: but we long for the everlasting peace of Jerusalem where all quarrels are at an end. All these are the services called out by men's needs. Remove distress, and there will be no place for works of mercy. Works of mercy will cease, but there will be no quenching of the fire of charity. You may have the truest love for a happy man, on whom you have nothing to bestow: such love will have a greater sincerity and a far more unspoilt purity. Once you

[139]

have bestowed gifts on the unfortunate, you may easily yield to the temptation to exalt yourself over him, to assume superiority over the object of your benefaction. He fell into need and you supplied him: you feel yourself as the giver to be a bigger man than the receiver of the gift. You should want him to be your equal, that both may be subject to the one on whom no favour can be bestowed.

St Augustine, *Homilies on I John*, VIII

'Freund in der Not' will nicht viel heißen;
Hilfreich möchte sich mancher erweisen,
Aber die neidlos ein Glück dir gönnen,
Die darfst du wahrlich 'Freunde' nennen.

'Friend in need' will not signify much;
Many a one would like to prove himself helpful,
But those who without envy will not grudge you a piece of good
    luck,
Those you may truly call 'friends'.

Paul von Heyse

Welcome the coming, speed the parting guest.

Alexander Pope (translating Homer's *Odyssey*, 15.84)

Keen, fitful gusts are whispering here and there
Among the bushes, half leafless and dry;
The stars look very cold about the sky,
And I have many miles on foot to fare.
Yet feel I little of the cool bleak air,
Or of the dead leaves rustling drearily,
Or of those silver lamps that burn on high,
Or of the distance from home's pleasant lair.
For I am brimful of the friendliness
That in a little cottage I have found;

Grace

Of fair-haired Milton's eloquent distress,
And all his love for gentle Lycid drowned;
Of lovely Laura in her light green dress,
And faithful Petrarch gloriously crowned.

John Keats

They told me, Heraclitus, they told me you were dead,
They brought me bitter news to hear and bitter tears to shed.
I wept as I remembered how often you and I
Had tired the sun with talking and sent him down the sky.

And now that thou art lying, my dear old Carian guest,
A handful of grey ashes, cold and long ago at rest,
Your pleasant voices are not dead, your nightingales yet wake;
For Death, though he takes all away, yet these he cannot take.

Callimachus, translation by William Cory, adapted by Ivo Mosley

. . . volsimi alla sinistra col rispitto
    col quale il fantolin corre alla mamma
    quando ha paura o quando elli è afflitto,
per dicere a Virgilio: 'Men che dramma
    di sangue m'e rimaso che non tremi:
    conosco i segni dell'antica fiamma.'
Ma Virgilio n'avea lasciati scemi
    di sè, Virgilio dolcissimo patre,
    Virgilio a cui per mia salute die'mi;
nè quantunque perdeo l'antica matre
    valse alle guance nette di rugiada,
    che, lacrimando, non tornasser atre.
'Dante, perchè Virgilio se ne vada,
    non piangier anco, non piangere ancora;
    chè pianger ti conven per altra spada.'

I turned me to the left with the trust with which the little child runs
to his mother when he is frightened or when he is afflicted, to say to
Virgil: 'Less than a drop of blood is left in me that trembleth not; I
recognise the tokens of the ancient flame.' But Virgil had left us
bereft of himself, Virgil sweetest father, Virgil to whom for my weal
I gave me up: nor did all that our ancient mother lost, avail to keep
my dew-washed cheeks from turning dark again with tears. 'Dante,
for that Virgil goeth away, weep not yet, weep not yet, for thou must
weep for another sword.'

Dante Alighieri, *Purgatorio*, Canto XXX, ll. 43–57

The going away of friends does not make the remainder more precious. It takes so much from them as there was a common link. A. B.
and C. make a party. A. dies. B. not only loses A.; but all A.'s part in
C. C. loses A.'s part in B., and so the alphabet sickens by subtraction
of interchangeables. I express myself muddily . . . I have a dulling
cold. My theory is to enjoy life, but my practice is against it.

Charles Lamb, Letter to William Wordsworth, 20 March 1822

Come back into memory, like as thou wert in the day-spring of thy
fancies, with hope like a fiery column before thee – the dark column
not yet turned – Samuel Taylor Coleridge – Logician,
Metaphysician, Bard!

Charles Lamb, *Essays of Elia*, 'Christ's Hospital five-and-thirty years ago'

Nor has the rolling year twice measured,
From sign to sign, its stedfast course,
Since every mortal power of Coleridge
Was frozen at its marvellous source;

The rapt One, of the godlike forehead,
The heaven-eyed creature sleeps in earth:

[142]

And Lamb, the frolic and the gentle,
Has vanished from his lonely hearth.

William Wordsworth, 'Extempore Effusion upon the death of James Hogg'

He first deceased; she for a little tried
To live without him, liked it not, and died.

Henry Wotton, 'Upon the death of Sir Albert Morton's wife'

The Victorians were stodgy in their moralizing but not in their love-making.

Nirad C.Chauduri, *Scholar extraordinary: The life of Professor the Rt Hon. Friedrich Max Müller, PC*, p. 151

My marriage was the most fortunate event of my life.

Edwin Muir, *An Autobiography*, p. 154

Between husband and wife friendship seems to exist by nature . . .

Aristotle, *Ethics*

John Anderson, my jo, John,
When we were first acquent,
Your locks were like the raven,
Your bonnie brow was brent;
But now your brow is beld, John,
Your locks are like the snow;
But blessings on your frosty pow,
John Anderson, my jo!

John Anderson, my jo, John,
We clamb the hill thegether;
And monie a canty day, John,

We've had wi'one anither:
Now we maun totter down John,
But hand in hand we'll go,
And sleep thegither at the foot,
John Anderson, my jo.

Robert Burns

And Elkanah, her husband, said to her, 'Hannah, why do you weep? And why do you not eat? And why is your heart sad? Am I not more to you than ten sons?'

1 Samuel 1.8

Blessed art thou, O Lord our God, King of the universe, who hast created all things to thy glory.
Blessed art thou, O Lord our God, King of the universe, Creator of man.
Blessed art thou, O Lord our God, King of the universe, who hast made man in thine image, after thy likeness, and hast prepared unto him, out of his very self, a perpetual fabric. Blessed art thou, O Lord, Creator of man.
May she who was barren be exceeding glad and exult, when her children are gathered within her in joy. Blessed art thou, O Lord, who makest Zion joyful through her children.
O make these loved companions greatly to rejoice, even as of old thou didst gladden thy creature in the garden of Eden. Blessed art thou, O Lord, who makest bride and bridegroom to rejoice.
Blessed art thou, O Lord our God, King of the universe, who hast created joy and gladness, bridegroom and bride, mirth and exultation, pleasure and delight, love, brotherhood, peace and fellowship.
Soon may there be heard in the cities of Judah, and in the streets of Jerusalem, the voice of joy and gladness, the voice of the bridegroom and the voice of the bride, the jubilant voice of bridegrooms from

their canopies, and of youths from their feasts of song. Blessed art thou, O Lord, who makest the bridegroom to rejoice with the bride.

Hebrew wedding blessing

... What, then, was Christ's concern – what is Christ's concern – in the weddings of his friends? We do not read that he laid down the law to them at that time, or told them their obligations – we read that he concerned himself with the supply of their wine . . .
It is not surprising at all, then, that Christ should begin his ministry at a wedding: for a true marriage is a special favour of God's grace, and a direct foretaste of heaven . . .
    . . . Christ, in his first miracle at Cana of Galilee, not only multiplies the wine of happiness, he also brings it about that the best wine is kept to the last . . . The new miracle of Christ's religion is the union of duty with delight; but the miracle of miracles, and masterpiece of wonders, is the keeping of the best wine to the last; and even that last is not an end, for, says Christ at the Supper, 'I will drink it new with you in the Kingdom of God.'

Austin Farrer, *A Celebration of Faith*, 'For a Marriage'

The voice of my beloved! behold, he cometh leaping upon the
    mountains, bounding over the hills.
My beloved is like a gazelle, or a young stag. Behold, there he
    stands behind our wall, gazing in at the windows, looking
    through the lattice.
My beloved speaks and says to me, 'Arise, my love, my fair one, and
    come away; for lo, the winter is past, the rain is over and gone.
The flowers appear on the earth, the time of singing has come, and
    the voice of the turtledove is heard in our land.
The fig tree puts forth its figs, and the vines are in blossom; they
    give forth fragrance.
Arise, my love, my fair one, and come away.

O my dove, in the clefts of the rock, in the covert of the cliff, let me
    see your face, let me hear your voice, for your voice is sweet, and
    your face is comely.

Catch us the foxes, the little foxes, that spoil the vineyards, for our
    vineyards are in blossom.'

My beloved is mine, and I am his: he pastures his flock among the
    lilies.

Until the day breathes and the shadows flee, turn, my beloved, be
    like a gazelle or a young stag upon rugged mountains.

                                       The Song of Solomon 2.8–17

About the dead hour o' the night
She heard the bridles ring;
And Janet was as glad at that
As any earthly thing.

And first gaed by the black, black steed,
And syne gaed by the brown;
But fast she gript the milk-white steed
And pu'd the rider down.

She's pu'd him frae the milk-white steed,
An' loot the bridle fa',
And up there rase an eldritch cry,
'True Tam Lin he's awa'!'

They shaped him in her arms twa
An aske but and a snake;
But aye she grips and hau'ds him fast
To be her warldis make.

They shaped him in her arms twa
But and a deer sae wild;
But aye she grips and hau'ds him fast
The father o' her child.

They shaped him in her arms twa
A hot iron at the fire;
But aye she grips and hau'ds him fast
To be her heart's desire.

They shaped him in her arms at last
A mother-naked man;
She cast her mantle over him,
And sae her love she wan . . .

Anonymous, 'Tam Lin', XLI–XLVII

'Is it something we shall be afraid of *too*?' Lucy asked. And Philip at once said, 'Oh, then she really did mean to come, did she? But she wasn't to if she was afraid. Girls weren't expected to be brave.'

'They *are*, here', said Mr. Noah, 'the girls are expected to be brave and the boys kind.'

'Oh', said Philip doubtfully. And Lucy said: 'Of course I meant to come. You know you promised.'

E. Nesbit, *The Magic City*, p. 163

I How well I know what I mean to do
    When the long dark autumn-evenings come
    And where, my soul, is thy pleasant hue?
    With the music of all thy voices, dumb
    In life's November too!

II I shall be found by the fire, suppose,
    O'er a great wise book as beseemeth age,
    While the shutters flap as the cross-wind blows
    And I turn the page, and I turn the page,
    Not verse now, only prose! . . .

    VII Look at the ruined chapel again
          Half-way up in the alpine gorge! . . .

   XVI Poor little place, where its one priest comes
          On a festa-day, if he comes at all,
          To the dozen folk from their scattered homes,
          Gathered within that precinct small
          By the dozen ways one roams – . . .

 XVIII It has some pretension too, this front,
          With its bit of fresco half-moon-wise
          Set over the porch, Art's early wont:
          'Tis John in the Desert, I surmise,
          But has borne the weather's brunt –

   XIX Not from the fault of the builder, though,
          For a pent-house properly projects
          Where three carved beams make a certain show,
          Dating – good thought of our architect's –
          'Five, six, nine, he lets you know . . .

 XXVII Think, when our one soul understands
          The great Word which makes all things new,
          When earth breaks up and heaven expands,
          How will the change strike me and you
          In the house not made with hands?

XXVIII Oh I must feel your brain prompt mine,
          Your heart anticipate my heart,
          You must be just before, in fine,
          See and make me see, for your part,
          New depths of the divine! . . .

XXXIV Silent the crumbling bridge we cross,
          And pity and praise the chapel sweet,

And care about the fresco's loss,
And wish for our souls a like retreat,
And wonder at the moss.

XXXV   Stoop and kneel on the settle under,
Look through the window's grated square:
Nothing to see! For fear of plunder
The cross is down and the altar bare,
As if thieves don't fear thunder.

XXXVI   We stoop and look in through the grate,
See the little porch and rustic door,
Read duly the dead builder's date;
Then cross the bridge that we crossed before,
Take the path again – but wait!

XXXVII   Oh moment, one and infinite!
The water slips o'er stock and stone;
The West is tender, hardly bright:
How grey at once is the evening grown –
One star, its chrysolite! . . .

LII   And to watch you sink by the fireside now
Back again, as you mutely sit
Musing by fire-light, that great brow
And the spirit-small hand propping it,
Yonder, my heart knows how!

LIII   So, earth has gained by one man the more,
And the gain of earth must be heaven's gain too;
And the whole is well worth thinking o'er
When autumn comes; which I mean to do
One day, as I said before.

Robert Browning, 'By the fireside'

Let me, if I may, be ever welcomed to my room in winter by a glowing hearth, in summer by a vase of flowers; if I may not, let me then
think how nice they would be, and bury myself in my work. I do not
think that the path to contentment lies in despising what we have
not got. Let us acknowledge all good, all delight that the world holds,
and be content without it.

C. S. Lewis (ed.), *George MacDonald Anthology*, p. 103

When in Rome, do as the Romans do.

Proverb

At Christmas I no more desire a rose
Than wish a snow in May's newfangled mirth;
But like of each thing that in season grows.

William Shakespeare, *Love's Labour Lost*, I.1

I own that I am disposed to say grace upon twenty other occasions in
the course of the day besides my dinner. I want a form for setting out
upon a pleasant walk, for a moonlight ramble, for a friendly meeting, or a solved problem. Why have we none for books, those spiritual repasts? – a grace before Milton; a grace before Shakespeare; a
devotional exercise proper to be said before reading the Fairy
Queen?

Charles Lamb, *Essays of Elia*, 'Grace before meat'

When that hour came to me among the pines, I wakened thirsty. My
tin was standing beside me half full of water. I emptied it at a
draught; and feeling broad awake after this internal cold aspersion,
sat upright to make a cigarette. The stars were clear, coloured, and
jewel-like, but not frosty. A faint silvery vapour stood for the Milky
Way. All around me the black fir-points stood upright and stock-still.

Grace

By the whiteness of the pack-saddle, I could see Modestine walking round and round at the length of her tether; I could hear her steadily munching at the sward; but there was not another sound, save the indescribable quiet talk of the runnel over the stones.

I hastened to prepare my pack, and tackle the steep ascent that lay before me; but I had something on my mind. It was only a fancy; yet a fancy will sometimes be importunate. I had been most hospitably received and punctually served in my green caravanserai. The room was airy, the water excellent, and the dawn had called me to a moment. I say nothing of the tapestries or the inimitable ceiling, nor yet of the view which I commanded from the window; but I felt I was in some one's debt for all this liberal entertainment. And so it pleased me, in a laughing way, to leave pieces of money on the turf as I went along, until I had left enough for my night's lodging. I trust they did not fall to some rich and churlish drover.

R. L. Stevenson, *Travels with a Donkey in the Cevennes*, p. 296

I arise today
Through a mighty strength, the invocation of the Trinity
Through belief in the threeness
Through confession of the oneness
Of the Creator of Creation.

I arise today
Through the strength of Christ's birth with His baptism,
Through the strength of His crucifixion with His burial,
Through the strength of His resurrection with His Ascension,
Through the strength of His coming down for Judgement.

I arise today
Through the strength of the love of Cherubim,
In obedience of angels,
In the service of archangels,

In prayers of ancestors,
In predictions of prophets,
In preachings of apostles,
In faith of confessors,
In deeds of righteous men.

I arise today
Through the strength of heaven; –
Light of sun,
Radiance of moon,
Splendour of fire,
Spread of lightning,
Swiftness of wind,
Depth of sea,
Stability of earth,
Firmness of rock.

I arise today
Through God's strength to pilot me,
God's might to uphold me,
God's wisdom to guide me,
God's hand to guard me,
God's shield to protect me,
God's host to save me,
From snares of devils,
From temptations of vices,
From all who shall wish me ill,
Afar and near,
Alone and in multitude.

I summon today all these powers between me and those evils,
Against every cruel merciless power that may oppose my body
    and soul,

Grace

Against incantations of false prophets,
Against black laws of pagandom,
Against spells of witches
Against every knowledge that corrupts man's body and soul.

Christ to shield me this day
So that there come to me abundance of reward.
Christ with me, Christ before me, Christ behind me,
Christ in me, Christ beneath me, Christ above me,
Christ when I lie down, Christ when I sit, Christ when I arise,
Christ in the heart of every man who thinks of me,
Christ in the mouth of everyone who speaks of me,
Christ in every eye that sees me,
Christ in every ear that hears me.

'St Patrick's Breastplate', translation by Kuno Meyer, from John V. Taylor
The Primal Vision

At the world's end to whom shall I tell the story?
A god came down, they say, from another heaven
Not in rebellion but in pity and love,
Was born a son of a woman, lived and died,
And rose again with all the spoils of time
Back to his home, where now they are transmuted
Into bright toys and various frames of glory;
And time itself is there a world of marvels.
If I could find that god, he would hear and answer.

Edwin Muir, 'Prometheus'

Καὶ ὁ Λόγοσ σὰρξ ε γένετο

And the Word was made flesh.

The Gospel according to St John 1.14

Have this mind among yourselves, which you have in Christ Jesus, who, though he was in the form of God, did not count equality with God a thing to be grasped, but emptied himself, taking the form of a servant, and being born in the likeness of men. And being found in human form he humbled himself and became obedient unto death, even death on a cross. Therefore God has highly exalted him, and bestowed on him the name which is above every name, that at the name of Jesus every knee should bow, in heaven, and on earth and under the earth, and every tongue confess that Jesus Christ is Lord, to the glory of God the Father.

St Paul's Epistle to the Philippians 2.5–11

The bells of waiting Advent ring,
The Tortoise stove is lit again
And lamp-oil light across the night
Has caught the streaks of winter rain
In many a stained-glass window sheen
From Crimson Lake to Hooker's Green.

The holly in the windy hedge
And round the Manor House the yew
Will soon be stripped to deck the ledge,
The altar, font and arch and pew,
So that the villagers can say
'The church looks nice' on Christmas Day.

Provincial public houses blaze
And Corporation tramcars clang,
On lighted tenements I gaze
Where paper decorations hang,
And bunting in the red Town Hall
Says 'Merry Christmas to you all'.

And London shops on Christmas Eve
Are strung with silver bells and flowers
As hurrying clerks the City leave
To pigeon-haunted classic towers,
And marbled clouds go scudding by
The many-steepled London sky.

And girls in slacks remember Dad,
And oafish louts remember Mum,
And sleepless children's hearts are glad,
And Christmas-morning bells say 'Come!'
Even to shining ones who dwell
Safe in the Dorchester Hotel.

And it is true? And is it true,
This most tremendous tale of all,
Seen in a stained-glass window's hue,
A Baby in an ox's stall?
The Maker of the stars and sea
Become a Child on earth for me?

And is it true? For if it is
No loving fingers tying strings
Around those tissued fripperies,
The sweet and silly Christmas things,
Bath salts and inexpensive scent
And hideous tie so kindly meant,

No love that in a family dwells,
No carolling in frosty air,
Nor all the steeple-shaking bells
Can with this single Truth compare –
That God was Man in Palestine
And lives today in bread and wine.

John Betjeman, 'Christmas'

Blessed art Thou, Lord our God, ruler of the universe, who brings forth bread from the earth.

Hebrew grace

And he said to them, 'Come away by yourselves to a lonely place, and rest a while.' For many were coming and going, and they had no leisure even to eat.

The Gospel according to St Mark 6.31

When he was at table with them, he took the bread and blessed, and broke it, and gave it to them.

The Gospel according to St Luke 24.30

I.1–II.1 At the holy table the people meet to worship God, and God is present to meet and bless his people. Here we are in a special manner invited to offer up to God our souls, our bodies, and whatever we can *give* and God offers to us the body and blood of his Son, and all the other blessings which we need to *receive*. So that the Holy Sacrament, like the ancient passover, is a great mystery, consisting both of *sacrament* and *sacrifice*; that is, of the religious *service* which the people owe to God, and of the full *salvation* which God hath promised to his people.

How careful, then, should every Christian be to understand, what so nearly concerns both his happiness and his duty! It was on this account, that the devil, from the very beginning, has been so busy about this Sacrament, driving men either to make it a *false god*, or an *empty ceremony*. So much the more let all who have either piety towards God, or any care of their own souls, so manage their devotions, as to avoid superstition on the one hand, and profaneness on the other.

The Lord's Supper was chiefly ordained for a sacrament. 1. To *represent* the sufferings of Christ which are past, whereof it is a

[156]

memorial: 2. To *convey* the first fruits of these sufferings, in *present graces*, whereof it is a means: and 3. To assure us of glory to come, whereof it is an infallible *pledge*.

II.9 My Lord and my God, I behold in this bread, made of corn that was cut down, beaten, ground, and bruised by men, all the heavy blows, and plagues, and pains, which thou didst suffer from thy murderers! I behold in this bread, dried up and baked with fire, the fiery wrath which thou didst suffer from above! My God, my God, why hast thou forsaken him! The violence of wicked men first hath made him a *martyr*, then the fire of heaven hath made him a *burnt-sacrifice*. And lo, he is become to me the 'bread of life'.

Let us go, then, to take and eat it.

Daniel Brevint, *The Christian Sacrament, and Sacrifice*

If anyone be in despair . . . let him go joyfully to the Sacrament . . . and seek help from the entire company of the spiritual body and say, 'I have on my side Christ's Righteousness, life and sufferings with all the holy angels and all the blessed in heaven and all good men upon earth. If I die I am not alone in death. If I suffer, they suffer with me.'

Martin Luther, 'On the blessed Sacrament'

Love is that liquor sweet and most divine,
Which my God feels as bloud, but I as wine.

George Herbert, 'The Agonie'

Was ever another command so obeyed? For century after century, spreading slowly to every continent and country and among every race on earth, this action has been done, in every conceivable human circumstance, for every conceivable human need from infancy and before it to extreme old age and after it, from the pinnacles of earthly greatness to the refuge of fugitives in the caves and dens of the earth. Men have found no better thing than this to do for kings at their crowning and for criminals going to the scaffold; for armies in triumph or for a bride and bridegroom in a little country church; for the proclamation of a dogma or for a good crop of wheat; for the wisdom of the Parliament of a mighty nation or for a sick old woman afraid to die; for a schoolboy sitting an examination or for Columbus setting out to discover America; for the famine of whole provinces or for the soul of a dead lover; in thankfulness because my father did not die of pneumonia; for a village headman much tempted to return to fetich because the yams had failed; because the Turk was at the gates of Vienna; for the repentance of Margaret; for the settlement of a strike; for a son for a barren woman; for Captain so-and-so, wounded and prisoner of war; while the lions roared in the nearby amphitheatre; on the beach at Dunkirk; while the hiss of scythes in the thick June grass came faintly through the windows of the church; tremulously by an old monk on the fiftieth anniversary of his vows; furtively, by an exiled bishop who had hewn timber all day in a prison camp near Murmansk; gorgeously, for the canonisation of S. Joan of Arc – one could fill many pages with the reasons why men have done this, and not tell a hundredth part of them. And best of all, week by week and month by month, on a hundred thousand successive Sundays, faithfully, unfailingly, across all the parishes of Christendom, the pastors have done this just to make the *plebs sancta Dei* – the holy common people of God.

Gregory Dix, The Shape of the Liturgy, p. 744

It does not matter where you bury my body. Do not let that worry you! All I ask of you is that, wherever you may be, you should remember me at the altar of the Lord.

St Augustine, Confessions, ix.ii (The death of St Monica)

His was the word that spake it,
He took the bread and brake it,
And what his word did make it,
I do believe and take it.

Queen Elizabeth I

And thou didst beat back the weakness of my sight, shining forth
upon me thy dazzling beams of light, and I trembled with love and
fear. I realised that I was far away from thee in the land of unlike-
ness, as if I heard thy voice from on high: 'I am the food of strong
men; grow and you shall feed on me; nor shall you change me, like
the food of your flesh into yourself, but you shall be changed into my
likeness.'

St Augustine, *Confessions*, VII.10

All my hope on God is founded;
He doth still my trust renew.
Me through change and chance he guideth,
Only good and only true.
   God unknown,
   He alone
Calls my heart to be his own.

Pride of man and earthly glory,
Sword and crown betray his trust;
What with care and toil he buildeth,
Tower and temple, fall to dust
   But God's power,
   Hour by hour,
Is my temple and my tower.

God's great goodness aye endureth,
Deep his wisdom, passing thought:
Splendour, light and life attend him,
Beauty springeth out of naught.
　　Evermore
　　From his store
New-born worlds rise and adore.

Daily doth th'Almighty giver
Bounteous gifts on us bestow;
His desire our soul delighteth,
Pleasure leads us where we go.
　　Love doth stand
　　At his hand;
Joy doth wait on his command.

Still from man to God eternal
Sacrifice of praise be done,
High above all praises praising
For the gift of Christ his Son.
　　Christ doth call
　　One and all:
Ye who follow shall not fall.

Robert Bridges

Peter seeing him saith to Jesus, Lord, and what shall this man do?
Jesus saith unto him, If I will that he should tarry till I come, what is
that to thee? Follow thou me.

The Gospel according to St John 21.21–2 (King James Version)

If we are unhappy with the ending of Mark's Gospel as he left it, it is
perhaps because we expect him to 'round it off' with an appearance

of the risen Lord . . . But is this, perhaps, because Mark is inviting us to make our own response? Is it because this was the starting-point for Mark's own readers? They could not go and inspect the tomb for themselves; they had to rely on the evidence of others that it was indeed empty. As for 'seeing' the risen Lord, that was a possibility for them all – not, indeed, in the special way reported by the other evangelists and by Paul, in the so-called 'resurrection appearances', but by accepting the invitation of the risen Lord to 'go to Galilee', the place of discipleship. The promise is intended for them – for us – as well as for the eleven frightened disciples: if you want to see Jesus, then follow where he leads. This is the end of Mark's story, because it is the beginning of discipleship.

Morna Hooker, The Gospel according to St Mark, p. 393

. . . You are not your own; you were bought with a price . . .

St Paul's First Epistle to the Corinthians 6.19–20

Almighty God, Father of all mercies, we thine unworthy servants do give thee most humble and hearty thanks for all thy goodness and loving-kindness to us, and to all men. We bless thee for our creation, preservation, and all the blessings of this life; but above all, for thine inestimable love in the redemption of the world by our Lord Jesus Christ; for the means of grace, and for the hope of glory. And, we beseech thee, give us that due sense of all thy mercies, that our hearts may be unfeignedly thankful, and that we show forth thy praise, not only with our lips, but in our lives; by giving up ourselves to thy service, and by walking before thee in holiness and righteousness all our days; through Jesus Christ our Lord, to whom with thee and the Holy Ghost be all honour and glory, world without end. *Amen.*

The Book of Common Prayer, A General Thanksgiving

Dying: creation's cost and how God has paid it

The more faith is strongly positive, the more it demands truthfulness about the troubles of the world. Such honesty is not rare. One way in which human beings have managed their fears and uncertainties is by expressing them profoundly.

For some believers, faith would be impossible unless it included the discovery that God does not stand aside from any of the sufferings of human creatures. Some troubles are worse than death but none is more certain. Honourable hope that creation is worthwhile after all is based on the paradox of a God who died.

'That I may be certified how long I have to live' – what a terrifying prayer! Lord, let me never be certified of anything of the kind.

D. L. Sayers, *The Nine Tailors*, p. 83

'He's dreaming now,' said Tweedledee, 'and what do you suppose he is dreaming about?'

Alice said, 'Nobody can guess that.'

'Why, about *you!*' Tweedledee, exclaimed, clapping his hands triumphantly. 'And if he left off dreaming about you, where do you suppose you'd be?'

[162]

'Where I am now, of course,' said Alice.

'Not you!' Tweedledee retorted contemptuously. 'You'd be nowhere. Why, you're only a sort of thing in his dream!'

'If that there King was to wake', added Tweedledum, 'you'd go out – bang! – just like a candle!'

'I shouldn't!' Alice exclaimed indignantly. 'Besides, if *I'm* only a sort of thing in his dream, what are *you*, I should like to know?'

'Ditto,' said Tweedledum.

'Ditto, ditto!' cried Tweedledee.

He shouted this so loud that Alice couldn't help saying 'Hush! You'll be waking him, I'm afraid, if you make so much noise.'

'Well, it's no use *your* talking about waking him,' said Tweedledum, 'when you're only one of the things in his dream. You know very well you're not real.'

'I *am* real!' said Alice, and began to cry.

'You won't make yourself a bit realler by crying,' Tweedledee remarked: 'there's nothing to cry about.'

'If I wasn't real', Alice said – half laughing through her tears, it all seemed so ridiculous – 'I shouldn't be able to cry.'

'I hope you don't think those are *real* tears?' Tweedledum interrupted in a tone of great contempt.

'I know they're talking nonsense,' Alice thought to herself: 'and it's foolish to cry about it.'

Lewis Carroll, *Through the Looking-Glass*, Chapter 4

The glories of our blood and state
Are shadows, not substantial things;
There is no armour against fate;
Death lays his icy hand on kings:
Sceptre and crown
Must tumble down,
And in the dust be equal made
With the poor crookèd scythe and spade.

Some men with swords may reap the field,
And plant fresh laurels where they kill:
But their strong nerves at last must yield;
They tame but one another still:
Early or late
They stoop to fate,
And must give up their murmuring breath
When they, pale captives, creep to death.

The garlands wither on your brow;
Then boast no more your mighty deeds!
Upon death's purple altar now
See where the victor-victim bleeds.
Your heads must come
To the cold tomb:
Only the actions of the just
Smell sweet, and blossom in their dust.

James Shirley, 'Death the Leveller'

Cast thy bread upon the waters: for thou shall find it after many days.
Give a portion to seven, and also to eight; for thou knowest not what
evil shall be upon the earth.
If the clouds be full of rain, they empty themselves upon the earth:
and if the tree fall toward the south, or toward the north, in the place
where the tree falleth, there it shall be.
He that observeth the wind shall not sow; and he that regardeth the
clouds shall not reap.
As thou knowest not what is the way of the spirit, nor how the bones
do grow in the womb of her that is with child: even so thou knowest
not the works of God who maketh all.
In the morning sow thy seed, and in the evening withhold not thine
hand: for thou knowest not whether shall prosper, either this or that,
or whether they both shall be alike good.

Truly the light is sweet, and a pleasant thing it is for the eyes to behold the sun:

But if a man live many years, and rejoice in them all; yet let him remember the days of darkness: for they shall be many. All that cometh is vanity.

Rejoice, young man, in thy youth; and let thy heart cheer thee in the days of thy youth, and walk in the ways of thine heart, and in the sight of thine eyes: but know thou, that for all these things God will bring thee into judgement.

Therefore remove sorrow from thy heart, and put away evil from thy flesh: for childhood and youth are vanity.

Remember now thy Creator in the days of thy youth, while the evil days come not, nor the years draw nigh, when thou shall say, I have no pleasure in them;

While the sun, or the light, or the moon, or the stars, be not darkened, nor the clouds return after the rain;

In the days when the keepers of the house shall tremble, and the strong men shall bow themselves, and the grinders cease because they are few, and those that look out of the windows be darkened.

And the doors shall be shut in the streets, when the sound of the grinding is low, and he shall rise up at the voice of the bird, and all the daughters of musick shall be brought low;

Also when they shall be afraid of that which is high, and fears shall be in the way, and the almond tree shall flourish, and the grasshopper shall be a burden, and desire shall fail: because man goeth to his long home, and the mourners go about the streets:

Or ever the silver cord be loosed, or the golden bowl be broken, or the pitcher be broken at the fountain, or the wheel broken at the cistern.

Then shall the dust return to the earth as it was: and the spirit shall return unto God who gave it.

Vanity of vanities, saith the preacher; all is vanity.

And moreover, because the preacher was wise, he still taught the people knowledge; yea, he gave good heed, and sought out, and set in order many proverbs.

The preacher sought to find out acceptable words: and that which was written was upright, even words of truth.

The words of the wise are as goads, and as nails fastened by the masters of assemblies, which are given from one shepherd.

And further, by these, my son, be admonished: of making many books there is no end; and much study is a weariness of the flesh.

Let us hear the conclusion of the whole matter: Fear God, and keep his commandments: for this is the whole duty of man.

For God shall bring every work into judgement, with every secret thing, whether it be good, or whether it be evil.

Ecclesiastes 11–12 (King James Version)

'Deh, quando tu sarai tornato al mondo,
    e riposato della lunga via,'
    seguitò il terzo spirito al secondo
'ricorditi di me che son la Pia:
    Siena mi fè; disfecemi Maremma:
    salsi colui che innanellata pria
disposando m'avea con la sua gemma.'

'Pray, when thou shalt return to the world, and art rested from thy long journey,' followed the third spirit after the second, 'remember me, who am La Pia. Siena made me, Maremma unmade me: 'tis known to him who, first plighting troth, had wedded me with his gem.'

Dante Alighieri, *Purgatorio*, V, ll. 130–6

I that in heill was and gladness
Am trublit now with great sickness
And feblit with infirmitie:–
    Timor Mortis conturbat me.

Dying

Our plesance here is all vain glory,
This fals world is but transitory,
The flesh is bruckle, the Feynd is slee:–
    Timor Mortis conturbat me.

The state of man doth change and vary,
Now sound, now sick, now blyth, now sary,
Now dansand mirry, now like to die:–
    Timor Mortis conturbat me.

No state in Erd now standeth sicker;
As with the wynd wavis the wicker
So wannis this world's vanitie:–
    Timor Mortis conturbat me.

Unto the ded gois all Estatis,
Princis, Prelatis, and Potestatis,
Baith rich and poor of all degree:–
    Timor Mortis conturbat me.

He taketh the knichtis in to the field
Enarmit under helm and scheild;
Victor he is at all mellie:–
    Timor Mortis conturbat me.

That strong unmerciful tyrand
Takis, on the motheris breast sowkand,
The babe full of benignitie:–
    Timor Mortis conturbat me.

He takis the campion in the stour,
The captain closit in the tour,
The lady in bour full of bewtie:–
    Timor Mortis conturbat me.

He spairis no lord for his piscence,
Na clerk for his intelligence;
His awful straik may no man flee:–
   Timor Mortis conturbat me.

Art-magicianis and astrologgis,
Rethoris, logicianis, and theologgis,
Them helpis no conclusions slee:–
   Timor Mortis conturbat me.

In medecine the most practicianis,
Leechis, surrigianis, and physicianis,
Themself fra ded may not supplee:–
   Timor Mortis conturbat me.

I see that makaris among the lave
Playis here their padyanis, syne gois to grave;
Sparis is nocht their facultie:–
   Timor Mortis conturbat me.

He has done petuously devour
The noble Chaucer, of makaris flour,
The Monk of Bury, and Gower, all three:–
   Timor Mortis conturbat me.

The good Sir Hew of Eglintoun,
Ettrick, Heriot, and Wintoun,
He has tane out of this cuntrie:–
   Timor Mortis conturbat me.

That scorpion fell has done infeck
Maister John Clerk, and James Afflek,
Fra ballat-making and tragedie:–
   Timor Mortis conturbat me.

Holland and Barbour he has berevit;
Alas! that he not with us levit
Sir Mungo Lockart of the Lee:–
  Timor Mortis conturbat me.

Clerk of Tranent eke he has tane,
That made the anteris of Gawaine;
Sir Gilbert Hay endit has he:–
  Timor Mortis conturbat me.

He has Blind Harry and Sandy Traill
Slain with his schour of mortal hail,
Quhilk Patrick Johnstoun might nought flee:–
  Timor Mortis conturbat me.

He has reft Merseir his endite,
That did in luve so lively write,
So short, so quick of sentence hie:–
  Timor Mortis conturbat me.

He has tane Rowll of Aberdene,
And gentill Rowll of Corstorphine;
Two better fallowis did no man see:–
  Timor Mortis conturbat me.

In Dumfermline he has done roun
With Maister Robert Henrysoun;
Sir John the Ross enbrast has he:–
  Timor Mortis conturbat me.

And he has now tane, last of a
Good gentil Stobo and Quintin Shaw,
Of quhom all wichtis hes pitie:–
  Timor Mortis conturbat me.

[169]

Profitable Wonders

Good Maister Walter Kennedy
In point of Death lies verily;
Great ruth it were that so suld be:–
    Timor Mortis conturbat me.

Sen he hath all my brether tane,
He will naught let me live alane;
Of force I man his next prey be:–
    Timor Mortis conturbat me.

Since for the Death remeid is none,
Best is that we for Death dispone,
After our death that live may we:–
    Timor Mortis conturbat me.

William Dunbar, 'Lament for the Makers'

O spare me a little, that I may recover my strength: before I go
hence, and be no more seen.

Psalm 39.15

What is this world? What asketh man to have?
Now with his love, now in his colde grave,
Alone withouten any companye.

Geoffrey Chaucer, *The Canterbury Tales*, 'The Knight's Tale'

Stop all the clocks, cut off the telephone;
Prevent the dog from barking with a juicy bone;
Silence the pianos and with muffled drum
Bring out the coffin, let the mourners come.

Let aeroplanes circle a-moaning overhead,
Scribbling on the sky the message 'He is dead.'

Dying

Put crêpe bows round the necks of the public doves;
Let the traffic policemen wear black cotton gloves.

He was my North, my South, my East, my West,
My working week and my Sunday rest;
My noon, my midnight, my talk, my song;
I thought that love could last for ever: I was wrong.

The stars are not wanted now, put out every one.
Pack up the moon and dismantle the sun;
Pour away the ocean, and sweep up the wood:
For nothing now can ever come to any good.

W. H. Auden

But where the greater malady is fix'd,
The lesser is scarce felt. Thou'dst shun a bear,
But if thy flight lay toward the roaring sea,
Thou'dst meet the bear i'the mouth. When the mind's free
The body's delicate; the tempest in my mind
Doth from my senses take all feeling else
Save what beats there.

William Shakespeare, *King Lear*, III.4

. . . but at my back I always hear
Time's wingèd chariot hurrying near;
And yonder all before us lie
Deserts of vast eternity.

Andrew Marvell, 'To his coy mistress'

Hope deferred makes the heart sick, but a desire fulfilled is a tree of
life.

Proverbs 13.12

VI
Well, and it was graceful of them – they'd break talk off
                                    and afford
– She, to bite her mask's black velvet – he to finger at
                                    his sword,
While you sat and played Toccatas, stately at the clavichord?

VII
What? Those lesser thirds so plaintive, sixths diminished, sigh
                                    on sigh,
Told them something? Those suspensions, those solutions –
                                    'Must we die?'
Those commiserating sevenths – 'Life might last! we can but try!'

VIII
'Were you happy?' – 'Yes' – 'And are you still as happy?' –
                                    'Yes. And you?'
– 'Then, more kisses!' – 'Did I stop them, when a million
                                    seemed so few?'
Hark, the dominant's persistence till it must be answered to!

IX
So, an octave struck the answer. Oh, they praised you, I
                                    dare say!
'Brave Galuppi! that was music! good alike at grave and gay!
I can always leave off talking when I hear a master play!'

X
Then they left you for their pleasure: till in due time,
                                    one by one,
Some with lives that came to nothing, some with deeds as
                                    well undone,
Death stepped tacitly and took them where they never see the sun.

Robert Browning, 'A Toccata of Galuppi's'

Dying

Iras: Finish, good lady, the bright day is done
      And we are for the dark.

William Shakespeare, *Antony and Cleopatra*, V.2

. . . No light, but rather darkness visible . . .

John Milton, *Paradise Lost*, I.63

Werd' ich zum Augenblicke sagen:
Verweile doch! du bist so schön!
Dann magst du mich in Fesseln schlagen,
Dann will ich gern zugrunde gehn!
Dann mag die Totenglocke schallen,
Dann bist du deines Dienstes frei,
Die Uhr mag stehn, der Zeiger fallen,
Es sei die Zeit für mich vorbei!

If to the moment I should say:
'O linger still! You are so fair!'
Then you may clasp me in your chain,
Then I will gladly be destroyed!
For then the passing-bell may toll,
Then from your service you are free,
The clock may stop, its hand shall fall,
And time for me be overpast!

Johann Wolfgang von Goethe, *Faust*, Part I

The best lack all conviction, and the worst
Are full of passionate intensity.

W. B. Yeats, 'The Second Coming'

Oh, cease! must hate and death return?
Cease! must men kill and die?
Cease! drain not to its dregs the urn
Of bitter prophecy.
The world is weary of the past,
Oh, might it die or rest at last!

Percy Bysshe Shelley, end of 'Hellas'

What passing-bells for these who die as cattle?
Only the monstrous anger of the guns.
Only the stuttering rifles' rapid rattle
Can patter out their hasty orisons.
No mockeries now for them; no prayers nor bells,
Nor any voice of mourning save the choirs, –
The shrill, demented choirs of wailing shells;
And bugles calling for them from sad shires.

What candles may be held to speed them all?
Not in the hands of boys, but in their eyes
Shall shine the holy glimmer of good-byes.
The pallor of girls' brows shall be their pall;
Their flowers the tenderness of patient minds,
And each slow dusk a drawing-down of blinds.

Wilfred Owen, 'Anthem for doomed youth'

He said to them, an enemy has done this.

The Gospel according to St Matthew 13.28

Look upon the covenant: for all the earth is full of darkness, and
cruel habitations.

Psalm 74.21

Dying

. . . that white anger of his victim's son
Shaking a fist at him with one fierce arm,
Signing himself with the other because of Christ
(Whose sad face on the cross sees only this
After the passion of a thousand years).

Robert Browning, 'Fra Lippo Lippi', ll. 153–7

If in that Syrian garden, ages slain,
You sleep, and know not you are dead in vain,
Nor even in dreams behold how dark and bright.
Ascends in smoke and fire by day and night
The hate you died to quench and could but fan,
Sleep on and see no morning, son of man.

But if, the grave rent and the stone rolled by,
At the right hand of majesty on high
You sit, and sitting there remember yet
Your tears, your agony and bloody sweat,
Your cross and passion and the life you gave,
Bow hither out of heaven and see and save.

A. E. Housman, 'Easter hymn'

You promise heavens free from strife,
Pure truth, and perfect change of will;
But sweet, sweet is this human life,
So sweet, I fain would breathe it still;
Your chilly stars I can forego,
This warm kind world is all I know.

William Cory, 'Minnermus in church'

Fear no more the heat o' the sun,
Nor the furious winter's rages;
Thou thy worldly task hast done,
Home art gone, and ta'en thy wages;
Golden lads and girls all must,
As chimney-sweepers, come to dust.

Fear no more the frown o' the great,
Thou art past the tyrant's stroke:
Care no more to clothe and eat;
To thee the reed is as the oak:
The sceptre, learning, physic, must
All follow this, and come to dust.

Fear no more the lightning-flash,
Or the all-dreaded thunder-stone;
Fear not slander, censure rash;
Thou hast finished joy and moan:
All lovers young, all lovers must
Consign to thee, and come to dust.

No exorciser harm thee!
Nor no witchcraft charm thee!
Ghost unlaid forbear thee!
Nothing ill come near thee!
Quiet consummation have
And renowned be thy grave!

William Shakespeare, *Cymbeline*, IV.2, 'Fidele'

Sweet day, so cool, so calm, so bright,
The bridall of the earth and sky:
The dew shall weep thy fall tonight;
     For thou must die.

Dying

Sweet rose, whose hue angrie and brave
Bids the rash gazer wipe his eye:
Thy root is ever in its grave,
  And thou must die.

Sweet spring, full of sweet dayes and roses,
A box where sweets compacted lie;
My musick shows ye have your closes,
  And all must die.

Onely a sweet and vertuous soul,
Like season'd timber, never gives;
But though the whole world turn to coal
  Then chiefly lives.

        George Herbert, 'Vertue'

The Sensitive Plant, like one forbid,
Wept, and the tears within each lid
Of its folded leaves, which together grew,
Were changed to a blight of frozen glue.

For the leaves soon fell, and the branches soon
By the heavy axe of the blast were hewn;
The sap sank to the root by every pore
As blood to a heart that will beat no more.

For Winter came: the wind was his whip:
One choppy finger was on his lip:
He had torn the cataracts from the hills
And they clanked at his girdle like manacles.

     Percy Bysshe Shelley, 'The Sensitive Plant', ll. 78–89

... Beauty that must die;
And Joy, whose hand is ever at his lips,
Bidding adieu ...

John Keats, 'Ode on Melancholy', III

The poplars are felled, farewell to the shade
And the whispering sound of the cool colonnade,
The winds play no longer, and sing in the leaves,
Nor Ouse on his bosom their image receives.

Twelve years have elapsed since I last took a view
Of my favourite field and the bank where they grew,
And now in the grass behold they are laid,
And the tree is my seat that once was my shade.

The blackbird has fled to another retreat
Where the hazels afford him a shade from the heat,
And the scene where his melody charmed me before,
Resounds with his sweet-flowing ditty no more.

My fugitive years are all hastening away,
And I must ere long lie as lowly as they,
With a turf on my breast, and a stone at my head,
Ere another such grove can arise in its stead.

'Tis a sight to engage me, if anything can,
To muse on the perishing pleasures of man;
Though his life be a dream, his enjoyments, I see,
Have a being less durable even than he.

William Cowper, 'The Poplar-Field'

Ah! yet doth beauty, like a dial-hand,
Steal from his figure, and no pace perceived.

William Shakespeare, Sonnet 104

Dying

. . . And ghastly thro' the drizzling rain
On the bald street breaks the blank day.

Alfred, Lord Tennyson, In Memoriam A.M.H., VII

. . . reluctance of the body to become a *thing* . . .

T. S. Eliot, The Cocktail Party, Act 3

When I have fears that I may cease to be
Before my pen has gleaned my teeming brain,
Before high-pilèd books, in charactery,
Hold like rich garners the full-ripened grain;
When I behold, upon the night's starred face,
Huge cloudy symbols of a high romance,
And think that I shall never live to trace
Their shadows with the magic hand of chance;
And when I feel, fair creature of an hour,
That I shall never look upon thee more,
Never have relish in the fairy power
Of unreflecting love; then on the shore
Of the wide world I stand alone and think
Till love and fame to nothingness do sink.

John Keats

The sun comes up, and many reptiles spawn
It sinks, and each ephemeral insect then
Is gathered into death without a dawn
And the immortal stars awake again.

Percy Bysshe Shelley, 'Adonais: an elegy on the death of John Keats'

I was thy neighbour once, thou rugged Pile! . . .

Ah! THEN, if mine had been the painter's hand,
To express what then I saw; and add the gleam,
The light that never was, on sea or land
The consecration, and the Poet's dream;

I would have painted thee, thou hoary Pile
Amid a world how different from this!
Beside a sea that could not cease to smile;
On tranquil land, beneath a sky of bliss.

William Wordsworth, 'Elegiac stanzas suggested by a picture of Peele Castle,
in a storm, painted by Sir George Beaumont', ll. 1, 13–20

– you and I are old;
Old age hath yet his honour and his toil;
Death closes all: but something near the end,
Some work of noble note, may yet be done,
Not unbecoming men that strove with Gods.
The lights begin to twinkle from the rocks:
The long day wanes: the slow moon climbs: the deep
Moans round with many voices. Come, my friends,
'Tis not too late to seek a newer world.
Push off, and sitting well in order smite
The sounding furrows; for my purpose holds
To sail beyond the sunset, and the baths
Of all the western stars, until I die.
It may be that the gulfs will wash us down:
It may be we shall touch the Happy Isles,
And see the great Achilles, whom we knew.

Alfred, Lord Tennyson, 'Ulysses'

Dying

The beauty of Israel is slain upon thy high places: how are the
 mighty fallen!

Tell it not in Gath, publish it not in the streets of Askelon; lest the
 daughters of the Philistines rejoice, lest the daughters of the
 uncircumcised triumph.

Ye mountains of Gilboa, let there be no dew, neither let there be
 rain, upon you, nor fields of offerings: for there the shield of the
 mighty is vilely cast away, the shield of Saul, as though he had
 not been anointed with oil.

From the blood of the slain, from the fat of the mighty, the bow of
 Jonathan turned not back, and the sword of Saul returned not
 empty.

Saul and Jonathan were lovely and pleasant in their lives, and in
 their death they were not divided: they were swifter than eagles,
 they were stronger than lions.

Ye daughters of Israel, weep over Saul, who clothed you in scarlet,
 with other delights, who put on ornaments of gold upon your
 apparel.

How are the mighty fallen in the midst of the battle!

O Jonathan, thou wast slain in thine high places.

I am distressed for thee, my brother Jonathan: very pleasant hast
 thou been unto me: thy love for me was wonderful, passing the
 love of women.

How are the mighty fallen, and the weapons of war perished!

2 Samuel 1.19, David's lament for Saul and Jonathan (King James Version)

My former thoughts returned: the fear that kills;
And hope that is unwilling to be fed;
Cold, pain, and labour, and all fleshly ills;
And mighty Poets in their misery dead.

William Wordsworth, 'Resolution and Independence'

Fear at my heart, as at a cup,
My life-blood seemed to sip!

Samuel Taylor Coleridge, 'The Rime of the Ancient Mariner', l. 205

Claudio: Ay, but to die, and go we know not where;
To lie in cold obstruction, and to rot;
This sensible warm motion to become
A kneaded clod; and the delighted spirit
To bathe in fiery floods, or to reside
In thrilling regions of thick-ribbèd ice;
To be imprisoned in the viewless winds,
And blown with restless violence round about
The pendant world; or to be worse than worst
Of those that lawless and incertain thoughts
Imagine howling; 'tis too horrible!
The meanest and most loathed worldly life
That age, ache, penury and imprisonment
Can lay on nature is a paradise
To what we fear of death.

William Shakespeare, *Measure for Measure*, III.I

Hence, viper thoughts, that coil around my mind
Reality's dark dream! I turn from thee and listen to the wind
Which long has raved unnoticed . . .

Samuel Taylor Coleridge, 'Dejection: an Ode', VII

Fear death? – to feel the fog in my throat,
The mist in my face,
When the snows begin, and the blasts denote
I am nearing the place,
The power of the night, the press of the storm,
The post of the foe;

[182]

Dying

Where he stands, the Arch Fear in a visible form,
Yet the strong man must go:
For the journey is done and the summit attained,
And the barriers fall,
Though a battle's to fight ere the guerdon be gained,
The reward of it all.
I was ever a fighter, so – one fight more,
The best and the last!
I would hate that death bandaged my eyes and forbore,
And bade me creep past.
No! let me taste the whole of it, fare like my peers
The heroes of old,
Bear the brunt, in a minute pay glad life's arrears
Of pain, darkness and cold.
For sudden the worst turns the best to the brave,
The black minute's at end,
And the elements' rage, the fiend-voices that rave,
Shall dwindle, shall blend,
Shall change, shall become first a peace out of pain,
Then a light, then thy breast,
O thou soul of my soul! I shall clasp thee again,
And with God be the rest!

Robert Browning, 'Prospice'

Your patient will, of course, have picked up the idea that he must
submit with patience to the Enemy's will. What the Enemy means
by this is primarily that he should accept with patience the tribulation which has actually been dealt out to him – the present anxiety
and suspense. It is about *this* that he is to say 'Thy will be done', and
for the daily task of bearing *this* that the daily bread will be provided.
It is your business to see that the patient never thinks of the present
fear as his appointed cross, but only of the things he is afraid of. Let
him regard them as his crosses: let him forget that, since they are

incompatible, they cannot all happen to him, and let him try to practice fortitude and patience to them all in advance. For real resignation, at the same moment, to a dozen different and hypothetical
fates, is almost impossible, and the Enemy does not greatly assist
those who are trying to attain it: resignation to present and actual
suffering, even when that suffering consists of fear, is far easier and
is usually helped by His direct action.

C. S. Lewis, *The Screwtape Letters*, 6

Nevertheless, though I am sometime afraid: yet put I my trust in
thee.

Psalm 56.3

Falstaff: I would it were bed-time, Hal, and all well.

William Shakespeare, *Henry IV Part I*, V.1

For lack of other comfort I lived on my courage, telling myself that
one never experiences all the good or all the evil that there is reason
to expect.

The Duke of Saint Simon, *Historical Memoirs*, II, 1710–15 (translated by Lucy Norton),
p. 128

All night long in a dream untroubled of hope
He brooded, clasping his knees.

Henry Newbolt, 'He Fell among Thieves'

He apologised to those who had stood round him all night for the
trouble which he had caused. He had been, he said, a most uncon-
scionable time dying; but he hoped that they would excuse it.

Charles II, in Lord Macaulay, *History of England*, I.IV, p. 342

Dying

Vae, puto deus fio

Alas, I think I am becoming a god.

Vespasian

'Io fui da Montefeltro, io son Buonconte:
   Giovanna o altri non ha di mi cura;
   per ch' io vo tra costor con bassa fronte.'
E io a lui: 'Quai forza o qual ventura
   ti traviò si fuor di Campaldino,
   che non si seppe mai tua sepultura?'
'Oh!' rispos'egli, 'a piè del Casentino
   traversa un'acqua che ha nome l'Archiano,
   che sopra l'Ermo nasce in Appenino.
Doue il vocabol suo divento vano,
   arriva' io forato nello gola,
   fuggendo a piede e 'nsanginuando il piano.
Quivi perdei la vista, e la parola;
   nel nome di Maria finii; e quivi
   caddi e rimase la mia carne sola.
Io dirò il vero, e tu il ridì tra i vivi:
   l'angel di Dio mi prese, e quel d'inferno
   gridava: 'O tu del ciel, perchè mi privi?'

'I was of Montefeltro; I am Buonconte; Giovanna, or any other hath
no care for me; wherefore I go among these, with downcast brow.'
   And I to him: 'What violence or what chance made thee stray so
far from Campaldino, that thy burial place ne'er was known?'
   'Oh,' answered he, 'at Casentino's foot a stream crosses, which is
named Archiano, and rises in the Apennines above the Hermitage.
There where its name is lost, did I arrive, pierced in the throat, flying

on foot, and bloodying the plain. There lost I vision, and ended my words upon the name of Mary; and there fell I, and my flesh alone was left. I will speak sooth, and do thou respeak it among the living; the angel of God took me, and one from Hell cried, "O thou from Heaven, wherefore robbest thou me?"'

Dante Alighieri, *Purgatorio*, V.88–105

The hand of the LORD was upon me, and he brought me out by the spirit of the LORD, and set me down in the midst of the valley; it was full of bones. And he led me round among them: and behold, there were very many upon the valley; and lo, they were very dry. And he said to me, 'Son of man, can these bones live?' And I answered, 'O Lord GOD, thou knowest.' Again he said to me, 'Prophesy to these bones, and say to them, O dry bones, hear the word of the LORD. Thus says the Lord GOD to these bones: Behold, I will cause breath to enter you, and you shall live. And I will lay sinews upon you, and will cause flesh to come upon you, and cover you with skin, and put breath in you, and you shall live; and you shall know that I am the LORD.'

So I prophesied as I was commanded; and as I prophesied, there was a noise, and behold, a rattling; and the bones came together, bone to its bone. And as I looked, there were sinews on them, and flesh had come upon them, and skin had covered them; but there was no breath in them. Then he said to me, 'Prophesy to the breath, prophesy, son of man, and say to the breath, Thus says the Lord GOD: come from the four winds, O breath, and breathe upon these slain, that they may live.' So I prophesied as he commanded me, and the breath came into them, and they lived, and stood upon their feet, an exceedingly great host.

Ezekiel 37.1–10

Dying

My first thought was, he lied in every word,
That hoary cripple, with malicious eye
Askance to watch the working of his lie
On mine, and mouth scarce able to afford
Suppression of the glee, that pursed and scored
Its edge, at one more victim gained thereby.

What else should he be set for, with his staff?
What, save to waylay with his lies, ensnare
All travellers who might find him posted there,
And ask the road? I guessed what skull-like laugh
Would break, what crutch 'gin write my epitaph
For pastime in the dusty thoroughfare,

If at his counsel I should turn aside
Into that ominous tract which, all agree,
Hides the Dark Tower. Yet acquiescingly
I did turn as he promised: neither pride
Nor hope re-kindling at the end descried,
So much as gladness that some end might be.

For, what with my whole world-wide wandering
What with my search drawn out thro' years, my hope
Dwindled into a ghost not fit to cope
With that obstreperous joy success would bring, –
I hardly tried now to rebuke the spring
My heart made, finding failure in its scope.

As when a sick man very near to death
Seems dead indeed, and feels begin and end
The tears and takes the farewell of each friend,
And hears one bid the other go, draw breath
Freelier outside, ('Since all is o'er', he saith,
'And the blow fallen no grieving can amend';)

While some discuss if near the other graves
Be room enough for this, and when a day
Suits best for carrying the corpse away,
With care about the banners, scarves and staves:
And still the man hears all, and only craves
He may not shame such tender love and stay.

Thus, I had so long suffered in this quest,
Heard failure prophesied so oft, been writ
So many times among 'The Band' – to wit,
The knights who to the Dark Tower's search addressed
Their steps – that just to fail as they, seemed best,
And all the doubt was now – should I be fit?

For mark! no sooner was I fairly found
Pledged to the plain, after a pace or two
Than, pausing to throw backward a last view,
O'er the safe-road, 'twas gone; grey plain all round:
Nothing but plain to the horizon's bound.
I might go on; nought else remained to do.

So, on I went. I think I never saw
Such starved ignoble nature; nothing throve:
For flowers – as well expect a cedar grove!
But cockle, spurge, according to their law
Might propagate their kind, with none to awe,
You'd think; a burr had been a treasure trove.

No! Penury, inertness and grimace,
In some strange sort, were the land's portion. 'See
Or shut your eyes', said Nature peevishly,
'It nothing skills: I cannot help my case:
'Tis the Last Judgment's fire must cure this place,
Calcine its clods and set my prisoners free.'

Dying

If there pushed any ragged thistle-stalk
Above its mates, the head was chopped; the bents
Were jealous else. What made those holes and rents
In the dock's harsh swarth leaves, bruised as to baulk
All hope of greenness? 'tis a brute must walk
Pashing their life out, with a brute's intents.

As for the grass, it grew as scant as hair
In leprosy; thin dry blades pricked the mud
Which underneath looked kneaded up with blood.
One stiff blind horse, his every bone astare,
Stood stupefied, however he came there:
Thrust out past service from the devil's stud!

Alive? he might be dead for aught I know,
With that red gaunt and colloped neck a-strain,
And shut eyes underneath the rusty mane;
Seldom went such grotesqueness with such woe;
I never saw a beast I hated so;
He must be wicked to deserve such pain.

I shut my eyes and turned them on my heart.
As a man calls for wine before he fights,
I asked one draught of earlier, happier sights,
Ere fitly I could hope to play my part.
Think first, fight afterwards – the soldiers' art:
One taste of the old time sets all to rights.

Not it! I fancied Cuthbert's reddening face
Beneath its garniture of curly gold,
Dear fellow, till I almost felt him fold
An arm in mine to fix me to the place,
That way he used. Alas, one night's disgrace!
Out went my heart's new fire and left it cold.

Giles then, the soul of honour – there he stands
Frank as ten years ago when knighted first.
What honest men should dare (he said) he durst.
Good – but the scene shifts – faugh! what hangman hands
Pin to his breast a parchment? His own bands
Read it. Poor traitor, spit upon and curst!

Better this present than a past like that;
Back therefore to my darkening path again!
No sound, no sight as far as eye could strain.
Will the night send a howlet or a bat?
I asked: when something on the dismal flat
Came to arrest my thoughts and change their train.

A sudden little river crossed my path
As unexpected as a serpent comes.
No sluggish tide congenial to the glooms;
This, as it frothed by, might have been a bath
For the fiend's glowing hoof – to see the wrath
Of its black eddy bespate with flakes and spumes.

So petty yet so spiteful! All along,
Low scrubby alders leaned down over it;
Drenched willows flung them headlong in a fit
Of mute despair, a suicidal throng:
The river which had done them all the wrong,
Whate'er that was, rolled by, deterred no whit.

Which, while I forded, – good saints, how I feared
To set my foot upon a dead man's cheek,
Each step, to feel the spear I thrust to seek
For hollows, tangled in his hair or beard!
– It may have been a water-rat I speared,
But, ugh! it sounded like a baby's shriek.

Dying

Glad was I when I reached the other bank.
Now for a better country. Vain presage!
Who were the strugglers, what war did they wage,
Whose savage trample thus could pad the dank
Soil to a plash? Toads in a poisoned tank,
Or wild cats in a red-hot iron cage –

The fight must so have seemed in that fell cirque.
What penned them there, with all the plain to choose?
No footprint leading to that horrid mews,
None out of it. Mad brewage set to work
Their brains, no doubt, like galley-slaves the Turk
Pits for his pastime, Christians against Jews.

And more than that – a furlong on – why, there!
What bad use was that engine for, that wheel,
Or brake, not wheel – that harrow fit to reel,
Men's bodies out like silk? with all the air
Of Tophet's tool, on earth left unaware,
Or brought to sharpen its rusty tooth of steel.

Then came a bit of stubbed ground, once a wood,
Next a marsh, it would seem, and now mere earth
Desperate and done with; (so a fool finds mirth,
Makes a thing and then mars it, till his mood
Changes and off he goes!) within a rood –
Bog, clay and rubble, sand and stark black dearth.

Now blotches rankling, coloured gay and grim,
Now patches where some leanness of the soil's
Broke into moss or substances like boils;
Then came some palsied oak, a cleft in him
Like a distorted mouth that splits its rim
Gaping at death, and dies while it recoils.

And just as far as ever from the end!
Nought in the distance but the evening, nought
To point my footsteps further! At the thought,
A great black bird, Apollyon's bosom-friend,
Sailed past, nor beat his wide wing dragon-penned
That brushed my cap – perchance the guide I sought.

For, looking up, aware I somehow grew,
'Spite of the dusk, the plain had given place
All round to mountains – with such name to grace
More ugly heights and heaps now stolen in view.
How thus they had surprised me, – solve it, you!
How to get from them was no clearer case.

Yet half I seemed to recognize some trick
Of mischief happened to me, God knows when –
In a bad dream perhaps. Here ended, then,
Progress this way. When, in the very nick
Of giving up, one time more, comes a click
As when a trap shuts – you're inside the den!

Burningly it came on me all at once,
This was the place! those two hills on the right,
Crouched like two bulls locked horn in horn in fight;
While to the left, a tall scalped mountain . . . Dunce,
Dotard, a-dozing at the very nonce,
After a life spent training for the sight!

What in the midst lay but the Tower itself?
The round squat turret, blind as the fool's heart,
Built of brown stone, without a counterpart
In the whole world. The tempest's mocking elf
Points to the shipman thus the unseen shelf
He strikes on, only when the timbers start.

Dying

Not see? because of night perhaps? why, day
Came back again for that! before it left,
The dying sunset kindled through a cleft:
The hills, like giants at a hunting, lay,
Chin upon hand, to see the game at bay, –
'Now stab and end the creature – to the heft!'

Not hear? when noise was everywhere! it tolled
Increasing like a bell. Names in my ears
Of all the lost adventurers my peers, –
How such a one was strong, and such was bold,
And such was fortunate, yet each of old
Lost, lost! one moment knelled the woe of years.

There they stood, ranged along the hill-sides, met
To view the last of me, a living frame
For one more picture! in a sheet of flame
I saw them and I knew them all. And yet
Dauntless the slug-horn to my lips I set,
And blew. '*Childe Roland to the Dark Tower came*'.

Robert Browning, 'Childe Roland to the Dark Tower came'

Milton, his face set fair for Paradise,
And knowing that he and Paradise were lost
In separate desolation, bravely crossed
Into his second night and paid his price.
Then towards the end he to the dark tower came
Set square in the gate, a mass of blackened stone
Crowned with vermilion fiends like streamers blown
From a great funnel filled with roaring flame.

Shut in his darkness, these he could not see,
But heard the steely clamour known too well
On Saturday nights in every street in Hell.
Where, past the devilish din, could Paradise be?
A footstep more, and his unblinded eyes
Saw far and near the fields of Paradise.

Edwin Muir, 'Milton'

O golden-tongued Romance, with serene lute!
Fair plumèd Siren, Queen of far-away!
Leave melodizing on this wintry day,
Shut up thine olden pages, and be mute.
Adieu! for, once again, the fierce dispute
Betwixt damnation and impassioned clay
Must I burn through, once more humbly assay
The bitter-sweet of this Shakespearian fruit.
Chief poet, and ye clouds of Albion,
Begetters of our deep eternal theme!
When through the old oak forest I am gone,
Let me not wander in a barren dream,
But when I am consumèd in the fire,
Give me new Phoenix wings to fly at my desire.

John Keats, 'On sitting down to read *King Lear* over again'

Whatever else you are doing, if you long for that sabbath, you are not ceasing to pray. If you do not want to cease praying, do not cease longing. Your unceasing desire is your unceasing prayer. You will lapse into silence if you lose your longing.

St Augustine, *Discourses on the Psalms*, Psalm 37
(Book of Common Prayer, Psalm 38.9)

Dying

When my devotions could not pierce
Thy silent ears;
Then was my heart broken, as was my verse;
My breast was full of fears,
         And disorder.

My bent thoughts, like a brittle bow,
Did fly asunder:
Each took his way; some would to pleasure go,
Some to the war and thunder
         Of alarms.

As good go anywhere, they say,
As to benumb
Both knees and heart, in crying night and day
Come, come, my God, O come
         But no hearing.

O that thou shouldst give dust a tongue
To cry to thee,
And then not hear it crying! all day long
My heart was in my knee.
         But no hearing.

Therefore my soul lay out of sight,
Untuned, unstrung;
My feeble spirit, unable to look right,
Like a nipped blossom, hung
         Discontented.

O clear and tune my heartless breast,
Defer no time;
That so thy favours granting my request
They and my mind may chime,
         And mend my rhyme.

George Herbert, 'Denial'

Verily thou art a God that hidest thyself, O God of Israel, the Saviour.

Isaiah 45.15 (Deutero-Isaiah)

Out of the deep have I called unto thee, O Lord: Lord, hear my
voice.
O let thine ears consider well: the voice of my complaint.
If thou, Lord, wilt be extreme to mark what is done amiss: O Lord,
who may abide it?
For there is mercy with thee: therefore shalt thou be feared.
I look for the Lord: my soul doth wait for him: in his word is my
trust.
My soul fleeth unto the Lord: before the morning watch, I say,
before the morning watch.
O Israel, trust in the Lord, for with the Lord there is mercy: and
with him is plenteous redemption.
And he shall redeem Israel: from all his sins.

Psalm 130

Our faith in the Creator is that he leaves no problem abandoned and
no evil redeemed.

We do not believe, of the children who died at Aberfan, that God
willed their deaths as a means to some greater good. If we so
believed, we should find that alleged 'good' tainted, compromised
and unacceptable: like Ivan Karamazov, we would have no part in it
and would 'hand in our ticket'. We believe that, at the moment when
the mountain of Aberfan slipped, 'something went wrong': the step
of creative risk was the step of disaster: the creative process passed
out of control . . . Our preaching on the Sunday after the tragedy was
not of a God who, from the top of the mountain, caused or permit-
ted, for his own inscrutable reasons, its disruption and descent; but

of One Who received, at the foot of the mountain, its appalling impact, and Who, at the extremity of endeavour, will find yet new resources to restore and to redeem.

W. H. Vanstone, *Love's Endeavour Love's Expense*, pp. 64–5

And he said, 'Go forth, and stand upon the mount before the Lord.' And behold, the Lord passed by, and a great and strong wind rent the mountains, and broke in pieces the rocks before the Lord, but the Lord was not in the wind; and after the wind an earthquake, but the Lord was not in the earthquake; and after the earthquake a fire, but the Lord was not in the fire; and after the fire a still small voice. And when Elijah heard it, he wrapped his face in his mantle and went out and stood at the entrance of the cave. And behold, there came a voice to him, and said, 'What are you doing here, Elijah?'

1 Kings 19.11–14

For he is not a man, as I am, that I might answer him, and that we should come to trial together. There is no umpire between us, who might lay his hand upon us both.

Job 9.32–3

Who hath believed our report? and to whom is the arm of the Lord revealed?
For he shall grow up before him as a tender plant, and as a root out of a dry ground: he hath no form nor comeliness; and when we shall see him, there is no beauty that we should desire him.
He is despised and rejected of men; a man of sorrows, and acquainted with grief: and we hid as it were our faces from him; he was despised, and we esteemed him not.
Surely he hath borne our grief, and carried our sorrows: yet we did esteem him stricken, smitten of God, and afflicted.

But he was wounded for our transgressions, he was bruised for our iniquities: the chastisement of our peace was upon him; and with his stripes we are healed.

All we like sheep have gone astray; we have turned every one to his own way; and the Lord hath laid upon him the iniquity of us all.

He was oppressed, and he was afflicted, yet he opened not his mouth: he is brought as a lamb to the slaughter, and as a sheep before her shearers is dumb, so he opened not his mouth. He was taken from prison and from judgment: and who shall declare his generation? for he was cut off out of the land of the living: for the transgression of my people was he stricken.

And he made his grave with the wicked, and with the rich in his death; because he had done no violence, neither was any deceit in his mouth.

Yet it hath pleased the Lord to bruise him; he hath put him to grief: when thou shalt make his soul an offering for sin, he shall see his seed, he shall prolong his days, and the pleasure of the Lord shall prosper in his hand.

He shall see of the travail of his soul, and shall be satisfied: by his knowledge shall my righteous servant justify many; for he shall bear their iniquities.

Therefore will I divide him a portion with the great, and he shall divide the spoil with the strong: because he hath poured out his soul unto death: and he was numbered with the transgressors; and he bare the sin of many, and made intercession for the transgressors.

Isaiah 53 (Deutero-Isaiah) (King James Version)

For one is approved if, mindful of God, he endures pain while suffering unjustly. For what credit is it, if when you do wrong and are beaten for it you take it patiently? But if when you do right and suffer for it you take it patiently, you have God's approval. For to this you have been called, because Christ also suffered for you, leaving you an example, that you should follow in his steps. He did no sin, no guile was found on his lips. When he was reviled, he did not revile in return; when he suffered, he did not threaten; but he trusted to him that judges justly. He himself bore our sins in his body on the tree, that we might die to sin and live to righteousness. By his wounds you have been healed. For you were straying like sheep, but have now returned to the Shepherd and Guardian of your souls.

The First Epistle of St Peter 2.19–25

Thou wast slain for me: and shall I leav thy Body in the feild O Lord? Shall I go away and be Merry, while the Love of my Soul and my only Lover is Dead upon the Cross.

Thomas Traherne, *Centuries*, I.89

Is it nothing to you, all ye that pass by? behold, and see if there be any sorrow like unto my sorrow.

Lamentations 1.12 (King James Version)

What exactly was Jesus like to meet? . . . Having asked this question, I looked at the Gospel again, and quite suddenly a new portrait seemed to stare at me out of the pages. I had never previously thought of a laughing, joking Jesus, physically strong and active, fond of good company and a glass of wine, telling funny stories, using, as every good teacher does, paradox and exaggeration as amongst the most effective aids to instruction, applying nicknames to his friends, and holding his companions spellbound with his talk. And yet, it is a very odd thing that we do not think of him in these terms. Granted that we are told to think of him as having every perfection of human nature, do we not ordinarily regard a sense of humour and high spirits as among the most desirable attributes a man can have? . . . The tragedy of the Cross was not that they crucified a melancholy figure, full of moral precepts, ascetic and gloomy. He was not John the Baptist, and the Baptist acknowledged this. What they crucified was a young man, vital, full of life and the joy of it, the Lord of life itself, and even more the Lord of laughter, someone so utterly attractive that people followed him for the sheer fun of it, someone much more like the picture of Dionysus in a Greek mosaic than the agonized and broken figure in a medieval cathedral, or the Christus Pantokrator of an orthodox monastery. The man of sorrows and acquainted with grief was in himself and before his passion utterly and divinely joyous.

Lord Hailsham, *The Door Wherein I Went*, p. 54

For John came neither eating nor drinking, and they say, He has a demon. The Son of man came eating and drinking, and they say, 'Behold a glutton and a drunkard, a friend of tax collectors and sinners!' But wisdom is justified by her deeds.

The Gospel according to St Matthew 11.18–19

Then the young Hero – it was God Almighty –
Strong and steadfast, stripped himself for battle;
He climbed up on the high gallows, constant in his purpose
Mounted it in the sight of many, mankind to ransom.

Anonymous, *The Dream of the Rood*

Chapter 22 We are his joy, we are his reward, we are his glory, we are his crown – and this was a special marvel and a thrilling vision, that we should be his crown. What I am describing causes Jesus such great pleasure that he thinks nothing of all his hardship and his bitter suffering and his cruel and shameful death. And in these words, 'If I could suffer more, I would suffer more', I truly saw that he was willing to die as often as he was able to die, and love would never let him rest until he had done it

Chapter 24 And with this our good Lord said most blessedly, 'Look how much I loved you'; as if he had said, 'My darling, look and see your Lord, your God, who is your maker and your eternal joy. See what pleasure and delight I take in your salvation, and for my love rejoice with me now.' And also, to make it plainer, these blessed words were said: 'Look how I loved you. Look and see that I loved you so much before I died for you that I was willing to die for you; and now I have died for you, and willingly suffered as much as I can for you. And now all my bitter torment and painful hardship has changed into endless joy and bliss for me and for you. How could it now be that you could make any request that pleased me that I would not very gladly grant you? For my pleasure is your holiness and your endless joy and bliss with me.' This is the meaning, as simply as I can explain it, of these blessed words, 'Look how much I loved you.' Our good Lord revealed this to make us glad and joyful.

Julian of Norwich, *Revelations of Divine Love*

O felix culpa, quae talem ac tantum meruit habere Redemptorem.

O happy fault, which has earned such a mighty Redeemer.

Roman Missal

My God, my God, look upon me; why hast thou forsaken me: and
    art so far from my health, and from the words of my complaint?
O my God, I cry in the day-time, but thou hearest not: and in the
    night-season also I take no rest.
And thou continuest holy: O thou worship of Israel.
Our fathers hoped in thee: they trusted in thee, and thou didst
    deliver them.
They called upon thee, and were holpen: they trusted in thee, and
    were not confounded.
But as for me, I am a worm, and no man: a very scorn of men, and
    the out-cast of the people.

All they that see me laugh me to scorn: they shoot out their lips,
and shake their heads, saying,

He trusted in God, that he would deliver him: let him deliver him,
if he will have him.

But thou art he that took me out of my mother's womb: thou wast
my hope, when I hanged yet upon my mother's breasts.

I have been left unto thee ever since I was born: thou art my God
even from my mother's womb.

O go not from me, for trouble is hard at hand: and there is none to
help me.

Many oxen are come about me: fat bulls of Basan close me in on
every side.

They gape upon me with their mouths: as it were a ramping and a
roaring lion.

I am poured out like water, and all my bones are out of joint: my
heart also in the midst of my body is even like melting wax.

My strength is dried up like a potsherd, and my tongue cleaveth to
my gums: and thou shalt bring me into the dust of death.

For many dogs are come about me: and the council of the wicked
layeth siege against me.

They pierced my hands and my feet; I may tell all my bones: they
stand staring and looking at me.

They part my garments among them: and cast lots upon my
vesture.

But be not thou far from me, O Lord: thou art my succour, haste
thee to help me.

Deliver my soul from the sword: my darling from the power of the
dog.

Save me from the lion's mouth: thou hast heard me also from
among the horns of the unicorns.

I will declare thy Name unto my brethren: in the midst of the
congregation will I praise thee.

O praise the Lord, ye that fear him: magnify him, all ye of the seed
of Jacob, and fear him, all ye seed of Israel;

For he hath not despised, nor abhorred, the low estate of the poor:
he hath not hid his face from him, but when he called unto him
he heard him.

My praise is of thee in the great congregation: my vows will I
perform in the sight of them that fear him.

The poor shall eat, and be satisfied: they that seek after the Lord
shall praise him; your heart shall live for ever.

All the ends of the world shall remember themselves, and be
turned unto the Lord: and all the kindreds of the nations shall
worship before him.

For the kingdom is the Lord's: and he is the Governor among the
people.

All such as be fat upon earth: have eaten, and worshipped.

All they that go down into the dust shall kneel before him: and no
man hath quickened his own soul.

They shall come, and the heavens shall declare his righteousness:
unto a people that shall be born, whom the Lord hath made.

Psalm 22

Rising: the faith that God can and will bring creation to good

'God with us' is only the beginning of an answer to the problem of evil. Everything would be in vain, unless the God who died is also the God who rose. This last section bears witness to the Christian hope that Christ did rise and that his rising is a pledge that the whole creation is to be reclaimed.

It is by illumination rather than by argument that faith is best nourished. Here are some examples of Christians offering what they have understood so far, and what has inspired them, to their fellow human beings as worthy of acceptance.

Do you not know that all of us who have been baptized into Christ Jesus were baptized into his death? We were buried therefore with him by baptism into death; so that as Christ was raised from the dead by the glory of the Father, we too might walk in newness of life. For if we have been united with him in a death like his, we shall certainly be united with him in a resurrection like his.

St Paul's Epistle to the Romans 6.3–5

I got me flowers to straw thy way;
I got me boughs off many a tree:
But thou wast up by break of day,
And brought'st thy sweets along with thee.

[204]

Rising

The Sunne arising in the East,
Though he give light, and th'East perfume;
If they should offer to contest
With thy arising, they presume.

Can there be any day but this,
Though many sunnes to shine endeavour?
We count three hundred, but we misse:
There is but one, and that one ever.

George Herbert, 'Easter'

They that sow in tears: shall reap in joy.
He that now goeth on his way weeping, and beareth forth good
seed: shall doubtless come again with joy, and bring his sheaves
with him.

Psalm 126.6–7

With this ambiguous earth
His dealings have been told us. These abide:
The signal to a maid, the human birth,
The lesson, and the young man crucified.

But not a star of all
The innumerable host of stars has heard
How he administered this terrestrial ball.
Our race have kept their Lord's entrusted word...

No planet knows that this
Our wayside planet, carrying land and wave,
Love and life multiplied, and pain and bliss,
Bears, as chief treasure, one forsaken grave.

Nor, in our little day,
May his devices with the heavens be guessed,
His pilgrimage to thread the Milky Way,
Or his bestowals there be manifest.

But, in the eternities,
Doubtless we shall compare together, hear
A million alien Gospels, in what guise,
He trod the Pleiades, the Lyre, the Bear.

O be prepared, my soul!
To read the inconceivable, to scan
The million forms of God those stars unroll
When, in our turn, we show to them a Man.

Alice Meynell, 'Christ in the universe'

He is the image of the invisible God, the first-born of all creation; for
in him all things were created, in heaven and on earth, visible and
invisible, whether thrones or dominions or principalities or author-
ities – all things were created through him and for him. He is before
all things, and in him all things hold together. He is the head of the
body, the church; he is the beginning, the first-born from the dead,
that in everything he might be pre-eminent. For in him all the fulness of God was pleased to dwell, and through him to reconcile to
himself all things, whether on earth or in heaven, making peace by
the blood of his cross.

St Paul's Epistle to the Colossians 1.15–21

And as for the dead being raised, have you not read in the book of
Moses, in the passage about the bush, how God said to him, 'I am
the God of Abraham, and the God of Isaac, and the God of Jacob? He
is not God of the dead, but of the living; you are quite wrong.'

The Gospel according to St Mark 12.26–7

Rising

Shall I put my hand upon the stone?
Would it be reverent? – superstitious? – or friendly?
I have brought no shekels for the expected offering.
How suitable, to come empty-handed,
And to find that *he is not here.*

Helen Oppenheimer, 'Holy Sepulchre (Day Excursion)'

What then shall we say to this? If God is for us, who is against us? He who did not spare his own Son, but gave him up for us all, will he not also give us all things with him? Who shall bring any charge against God's elect? It is God who justifies; who is to condemn? Is it Christ Jesus who died, yes, who was raised from the dead, who is at the right hand of God, who indeed intercedes for us? Who shall separate us from the love of Christ? Shall tribulation, or distress, or persecution, or famine, or nakedness, or peril, or sword? As it is written, 'For thy sake we are being killed all the day long; we are regarded as sheep to be slaughtered.' No, in all these things we are more than conquerors through him who loved us. For I am sure that neither death, nor life, nor angels, nor principalities, nor things present, nor things to come, nor powers, nor height, nor depth, nor anything else in all creation, will be able to separate us from the love of God in Christ Jesus our Lord.

St Paul's Epistle to the Romans 8.31–9

Space is a web of interactions between material energies which form a system by thus interacting. Unless the beings or energies of which heaven is composed are of a sort to interact physically with the energies in our physical world, heaven can be as dimensional as it likes, without ever getting pulled into our spatial field, or having any possible contact with us of any physical kind. There may well be contacts which are not physical at all between earthly minds and heavenly minds, but that's another story. How I wish we could explain the Einsteinian theory to St Augustine! Obviously his heaven is dimensional; but the stuff of glory which composes its constituents is surely not apt to interact with sticks and stones, with flesh and blood.

Austin Farrer, *Saving Belief*, p. 145

Now I would remind you, brethren, in what terms I preached to you the gospel, which you received, in which you stand, by which you are saved, if you hold it fast – unless you believed in vain.

For I delivered to you as of first importance what I also received, that Christ died for our sins in accordance with the scriptures, that he was buried, that he was raised on the third day in accordance with the scriptures, and that he appeared to Cephas, then to the twelve. Then he appeared to more than five hundred brethren at once, most of whom are still alive, though some have fallen asleep. Then he appeared to James, then to all the apostles. Last of all, as to one untimely born, he appeared also to me. For I am the least of all the apostles, unfit to be called an apostle, because I persecuted the church of God. But by the grace of God I am what I am, and his grace toward me was not in vain. On the contrary, I worked harder than any of them, though it was not I but the grace of God which is with me. Whether then it was I or they, so we preach and so you believed.

Now if Christ is preached as raised from the dead, how can some of you say that there is no resurrection of the dead? But if there is no resurrection of the dead, then Christ has not been raised; if Christ has not been raised, then our preaching is in vain and your faith is in vain. We are even found to be misrepresenting God, because we testified of God that he raised Christ, whom he did not raise if it is true that the dead are not raised. For if the dead are not raised, then Christ has not been raised. If Christ has not been raised, your faith is futile and you are still in your sins. Then those also who have fallen asleep in Christ have perished. If for this life only we have hoped in Christ, we are of all men most to be pitied.

But in fact Christ has been raised from the dead, the first fruits of those who have fallen asleep. For as by a man came death, by a man has come also the resurrection of the dead. For as in Adam all die, so also in Christ shall all be made alive. But each in his own order: Christ the first fruits, then at his coming those who belong to Christ. Then comes the end, when he delivers the kingdom to God the Father after destroying every rule and every authority and power. For he must reign until he has put all his enemies under his feet. The last enemy to be destroyed is death. 'For God has put all things in subjection under his feet.' But when it says, 'All things are put in subjection under him,' it is plain that he is excepted who put all things in subjection under him. When all things are subjected to him, then the Son himself will also be subjected to him who put all things under him, that God may be everything to every one.

Otherwise, what do people mean by being baptized on account of the dead? If the dead are not raised at all, why are people baptized on their behalf? Why am I in peril every hour? I protest, brethren, by my pride in you which I have in Christ Jesus our Lord, I die every day! What do I gain if, humanly speaking, I fought with wild beasts at Ephesus? If the dead are not raised, 'Let us eat and drink, for tomorrow we die.' Do not be deceived: 'Bad company ruins good morals.' Come to your right mind, and sin no more. For some have no knowledge of God. I say this to your shame.

But someone will ask, 'How are the dead raised? With what kind of body do they come?' You foolish man! What you sow does not come to life unless it dies. And what you sow is not the body which is to be, but a bare kernel, perhaps of wheat or of some other grain. But God gives it a body as he has chosen, and to each kind of seed its own body. For not all flesh is alike, but there is one kind for men, another for animals, another for birds, and another for fish. There are celestial bodies and there are terrestrial bodies; but the glory of the celestial is one, and the glory of the terrestrial is another. There is one glory of the sun, and another glory of the moon, and another glory of the stars; for star differs from star in glory.

So it is with the resurrection of the dead. What is sown is perishable, what is raised is imperishable. It is sown in dishonour, it is raised in glory. It is sown in weakness, it is raised in power. It is sown a physical body, it is raised a spiritual body. If there is a physical body, there is also a spiritual body. Thus it is written, 'The first man Adam became a living being'; the last Adam became a life-giving spirit. But it is not the spiritual which is first but the physical, and then the spiritual. The first man was from the earth, a man of dust; the second man is from heaven. As was the man of dust, so are those who are of the dust; and as is the man of heaven, so are those who are of heaven. Just as we have borne the image of the man of dust, we shall also bear the image of the man of heaven. I tell you this, brethren: flesh and blood cannot inherit the kingdom of God, nor does the perishable inherit the imperishable. Lo! I tell you a mystery. We shall not all sleep, but we shall all be changed, in a moment, in the twinkling of an eye, at the last trumpet. For the trumpet will sound, and the dead will be raised incorruptible, and we shall be changed. For this perishable nature must put on the imperishable, and this mortal nature must put on immortality. When the perishable puts on the imperishable, and the mortal puts on immortality, then shall come to pass the saying that is written, 'Death is swallowed up in victory.' 'O death, where is thy victory? O grave, where is thy sting?' The sting of death is sin, and the power of sin is the law. But thanks be to God, who gives us the victory through our Lord Jesus Christ.

St Paul's First Epistle to the Corinthians 15

This was a ravishing sight and a restful showing, that it is so everlastingly. And it is very pleasing to God and extremely helpful to us that we should see this while we are here. And the soul which sees it in this way makes itself like the one seen and unites itself to him in rest and peace through his grace. And it was a very great joy and bliss to me that I saw him sitting, for the certainty that he sits shows that he dwells there eternally. And he gave me certain knowledge that it was he who had shown me all that went before. And when I had considered this carefully, our good Lord gently revealed words to me, without any voice or opening of his lips, just as he had done before, and he said very lovingly, 'Know well now that what you saw today was no delirium; accept and believe it, hold to it and comfort yourself with it and trust to it, and you shall not be overcome.' These last words were said to prove to me with full assurance that it is our Lord Jesus who showed me everything. And just as in the first phrase which our good Lord revealed, referring to his blessed Passion – 'By this is the Fiend overcome' – in just the same way he said his last phrase with very great certainty, referring to all of us, 'You shall not be overcome.'

And all this teaching of true comfort applies without exception to all my fellow Christians, as I said before, and it is God's will that it should be so. And these words, 'You shall not be overcome', were said very loudly and clearly for security and comfort against all the tribulations that may come. He did not say, 'You shall not be tormented, you shall not be troubled, you shall not be grieved', but he said, 'You shall not be overcome.' God wants us to pay attention to these words and wants our trust always to be sure and strong, in weal and woe; for he loves and is pleased with us, and so he wishes us to love and be pleased with him and put great trust in him; and all shall be well.

And soon after this it was all over and I saw no more.

Julian of Norwich, *Revelations of Divine Love*, Chapter 68

Post tenebras spero lucem.

After the darkness I hope for the light.

On the tomb of Theresa Pelzer, Santa Maria del Popolo, Rome

. . . heaviness may endure for a night, but joy cometh in the
morning.

Psalm 30.5

. . . Never to be again! But many more of the kind
As good, nay, better perchance: is this your comfort to me?
To me, who must be saved because I cling with my mind
To the same, same self, same love, same God: ay, what was, shall
    be.

Therefore to whom turn I but to thee, the ineffable Name?
Builder and maker, thou, of houses not made with hands!
What, have fear of change from thee who art ever the same?
Doubt that thy power can fill the heart that thy power expands?

There shall never be one lost good! What was, shall live as
    before;
The evil is null, is nought, is silence implying sound;
What was good shall be good, with, for evil, so much good more;
On the earth the broken arcs; in the heaven, a perfect round.

All we have willed or hoped or dreamed of good shall exist;
Not its semblance, but itself; no beauty, nor good, nor power
Whose voice has gone forth, but each survives for the melodist
When eternity affirms the conception of an hour.

The high that proved too high, the heroic for earth too hard,
The passion that left the ground to lose itself in the sky,
Are music sent up to God by the lover and the bard;
Enough that he heard it once: we shall hear it by-and-by . . .

Robert Browning, 'Abt Vogler' (after he has been extemporizing upon
the musical instrument of his invention)

... But he will come again, it's said, though not
Unwanted and unsummoned; for all things,
Beasts of the field, and woods, and rocks, and seas,
And all mankind from end to end of the earth
Will call him with one voice. In our own time,
Some say, or at a time when time is ripe.
Then he will come, Christ the uncrucified,
Christ the discrucified, his death undone,
His agony unmade, his cross dismantled –
Glad to be so – and the tormented wood
Will cure its hurt and grow into a tree
In a green springing corner of young Eden,
And Judas damned take his long journey backward
From darkness into light and be a child
Beside his mother's knee, and the betrayal
Be quite undone and never more be done.

Edwin Muir, 'The Transfiguration'

For you did not receive the spirit of slavery to fall back into fear, but you have received the Spirit of sonship. When we cry, 'Abba, Father!' it is the Spirit himself bearing witness with our spirit that we are children of God, and if children, then heirs, heirs of God, and fellow heirs with Christ, provided we suffer with him in order that we may also be glorified with him.

I consider that the sufferings of this present time are not worth comparing with the glory that is to be revealed to us. For the creation waits with eager longing for the revealing of the sons of God; for the creation was subjected to futility, not of its own will but by the will of him who subjected it in hope; because the creation itself will be set free from its bondage to decay and obtain the glorious liberty of the children of God. We know that the whole creation has been groaning in travail together until now; and not only the creation, but we

ourselves, who have the first fruits of the Spirit, groan inwardly as
we wait for adoption as sons, the redemption of our bodies.

St Paul's Epistle to the Romans 8.15–23

Then the eyes of the blind shall be opened, and the ears of the deaf
shall be unstopped.
Then shall the lame man leap as an hart, and the tongue of the dumb
sing: for in the wilderness shall waters break out, and streams in the
desert.
And the parched ground shall become a pool, and the thirsty land
springs of water: in the habitation of dragons, where each lay, shall
be grass with reeds and rushes.
And an highway shall be there, and a way, and it shall be called the
way of holiness; the unclean shall not pass over it; but it shall be for
those: the wayfaring men, though fools, shall not err therein.
No lion shall be there, nor any ravenous beast shall go up thereon, it
shall not be found there; but the redeemed shall walk there:
And the ransomed of the Lord shall return, and come to Zion with
songs and everlasting joy upon their heads: they shall obtain joy and
gladness, and sorrow and sighing shall flee away.

Isaiah 35.5–10 (King James Version)

The voice of him that crieth in the wilderness, Prepare ye the way of
the Lord, make straight in the desert a highway for our God.
Every valley shall be exalted, and every mountain and hill shall be
made low: and the crooked shall be made straight, and the rough
places plain:
And the glory of the Lord shall be revealed, and all flesh shall see it
together: for the mouth of the Lord hath spoken it.

Isaiah 40.3–6 (Deutero-Isaiah) (King James Version)

Rising

Die unbegreiflich hohen Werke
Sind herrlich wie am ersten Tag.

The inconceivably high works
Are glorious as on the first day.

Johann Wolfgang von Goethe, *Faust*, 'Prolog im Himmel'

One foot in Eden still, I stand
And look across the other land.
The world's great age is growing late,
Yet strange these fields that we have planted
So long with crops of love and hate.
Time's handiworks by time are haunted,
And nothing now can separate
The corn and tares compactly grown.
The armorial weed in stillness bound
About the stalk; these are our own.
Evil and good stand thick around
In the fields of charity and sin
Where we shall lead our harvest in.

Yet still from Eden springs the root
As clean as on the starting day.
Time takes the foliage and the fruit
And burns the archetypal leaf
To shapes of terror and of grief
Scattered along the winter way.
But famished field and blackened tree
Bear flowers in Eden never known.
Blossoms of grief and charity
Bloom in these darkened fields alone.
What had Eden ever to say
Of hope and faith and pity and love

Until was buried all its day
And memory found its treasure trove?
Strange blessings never in Paradise
Fall from these beclouded skies.

Edwin Muir

But Jesus, who in this vision informed me of all that I needed to
know, answered with this assurance: 'Sin is befitting, but all shall be
well, and all shall be well, and all manner of things shall be well.'

Julian of Norwich, *Revelations of Divine Love*, Chapter 27

Thy mercy, O Lord, reacheth unto the heavens: and thy faithfulness
    unto the clouds.
Thy righteousness standeth like the strong mountains: thy
    judgments are like the great deep.
Thou, Lord, shalt save both man and beast; how excellent is thy
    mercy, O God: and the children of men shall put their trust
    under the shadow of thy wings.
They shall be satisfied with the plenteousness of thy house: and
    thou shalt give them drink of thy pleasures, as out of the river.
For with thee is the well of life: and in thy light shall we see light.

Psalm 36

So then, there remains a sabbath rest for the people of God.

The Epistle to the Hebrews 4.9

Vincendo me col lume d'un sorriso,
    ella mi disse: 'Volgiti ed ascolta,
    chè non pur ne' miei occhi è Paradiso.'

Rising

O'ercoming me with the light of a smile, she said to me: 'Turn thee, and hearken, for not only in my eyes is Paradise.'

Dante Alighieri, *Paradiso*, XVIII.19–21

Thou shalt show me the path of life; in thy presence is the fulness of joy: and at thy right hand is pleasure for evermore.

Psalm 16.12

Love bade me welcome: yet my soul drew back,
    Guiltie of dust and sinne.
But quick-ey'd Love, observing me grow slack
    From my first entrance in,
Drew nearer to me, sweetly questioning,
    If I lack'd any thing.

A guest, I answer'd, worthy to be here:
    Love said, You shall be he.
I, the unkinde, ungratefull? Ah my deare,
    I cannot look on thee.
Love took my hand, and smiling did reply,
    Who made the eyes but I?

Truth Lord, but I have marr'd them; let my shame
    Go where it doth deserve.
And know you not, sayes Love, who bore the blame?
    My deare, then I will serve.
You must sit down, sayes Love, and taste my meat.
    So I did sit and eat.

George Herbert, 'Love bade me welcome'

Profitable Wonders

Welcome one another, therefore, as Christ has welcomed you, for the glory of God.

St Paul's Epistle to the Romans 15.7

In unexperienced infancy
Many a sweet mistake doth lie –
Mistake, though false, intending true,
A seeming somewhat more than view –
That doth instruct the mind
In things that lie behind
And many secrets to us show
Which afterwards we come to know.

Thus did I by the water's brink
Another world beneath me think;
And while the lofty spacious skies
Reversèd there abused mine eyes,
I fancied other feet
Came mine to touch and meet;
As by some puddle I did play
Another world within it lay.

Beneath the water people drowned;
Yet with another heaven crowned,
In spacious regions seemed to go,
Freely moving to and fro.
In bright and open space
I saw their very face;
Eyes, hands and feet, they had like mine;
Another sun did with them shine.

'Twas strange that people there should walk,
And yet I could not hear them talk;

Rising

That through a little watery chink,
Which one dry ox or horse might drink,
We other worlds should see,
Yet not admitted be;
And other confines there behold
Of light and darkness, heat and cold.

I called them oft, but called in vain;
No speeches we could entertain;
Yet did I there expect to find
Some other world, to please my mind.
I plainly saw by these
A new Antipodes,
Whom, though they were so plainly seen
A film kept off that stood between.

By walking men's reversèd feet
I chanced another world to meet;
Though it did not to view exceed
A phantasm, 'tis a view indeed,
Where skies beneath us shine,
And earth by art divine
Another face presents below
Where people's feet against ours go.

Within the regions of the air,
Compassed about with heavens fair,
Great tracts of land there may be found
Enriched with fields and fertile ground;
Where many numerous hosts
In those far distant coasts,
For other great and glorious ends,
Inhabit, my yet unknown friends.

Profitable Wonders

Oh ye that stand upon the brink,
Whom I so near me, through the chink,
With wonder see, what faces there,
Whose feet, whose bodies, do ye wear?
I my companions see,
In you, another me.
They seemèd others, but are we;
Our second selves these shadows be.

Look, how far off these unknown skies
Extend themselves! Scarce with mine eyes
I can them reach. Oh ye my friends,
What Secret borders on those ends?
Are lofty heavens hurled
'Bout your inferior world?
Are ye the representatives
Of other people's distant lives?

Of all the playmates which I know
That here I do the image view
In other selves, what can it mean?
But that below the purling stream
Some unknown Joys there be
Laid up in store for me;
To which I shall, when that thin skin
Is broken, be admitted in.

Thomas Traherne, 'Shadows in the water'

. . . my readers, who will see in the tell-tale compression of the pages
before them, that we are all hastening together to perfect felicity.

Jane Austen, *Northanger Abbey*, Chapter 16

It is a curious fact that the conventional idea of Heaven, produced by people for the most part morbidly absorbed in morals, is a state of being in which art will be the only activity. Heaven to them is music, and music which they will all know by heart, like Church hymns. But a decent state of being cannot be all art any more than all morals.

If we think of Heaven as a real place it is as a heaven of real people doing real things.

A. Clutton Brock, *Immortality*, 'A Dream of Heaven', pp. 224, 225

I have often thought to myself that I know that I should want eternal life because I am told that God promises it to me and of course it is impolite not to want what God promises. But I have often wondered whether going on and on wouldn't be an awful bore. Of course, if we went on and on as we are now we should soon discover, as Sartre put it, that hell is other people. We only have to look in a mirror to see that unless we are transformed, heaven will be hell, supposing we spend our lives there. That is why it must be transformation, growth and development. But I have begun to get glimpses, especially through other people, that eternity could be infinitely worth it precisely because there will always be more to discover.

One way in which I picked this up was when I worked for the World Council of Churches and got increasingly frustrated over the language problem. How do you share communications with people who speak languages other than your own? There is a frustration over having to have everything conducted in most international gatherings in English, which is other people's second or third language. And that is particularly a frustration to me, with a Welsh ancestry, so that I rapidly get intoxicated by the exuberance of my own verbosity and go faster, with the result that communication becomes very difficult. It occurred to me that one of the purposes of eternity is to be enabled by the grace of God to learn perfectly every possible language there is, so that everyone can express themselves in such a way that they will be understood fully by other people and be able to share with other people. And there, as Humpty Dumpty might say, there is glory for you. There is an eternal possibility. So I am quite clear that heaven will not be a bore, because the mystery is infinite and there will always be more to discover.

David Jenkins, *God, Jesus and Life in the Spirit*, pp. 38–9

He that is in all, and with all, can never be Desolat. All the Joys and all the Treasures, all the Counsels and all the Perfections all the Angels and all the Saints of GOD are with Him. All the Kingdoms of the World and the Glory of them are continualy in his Ey: The Patriarchs Prophets and Apostles are always before Him. The Counsels and the fathers, the Bishops and the Doctors minister unto Him. All Temples are Open before Him, The Melodie of all Quires reviveth Him, the Learning of all Universities doth employ Him, the Riches of all Palaces Delight Him, The Joys of Eden Ravish Him, The Revelations of St John Transport Him, The Creation and the Day of Judgment pleas Him, The Hosannas of the Church Militant, and the Hallelujahs of the Saints Triumphant fill Him, The Splendor of all Coronations entertain Him, The Joys of Heaven surround Him, And our Saviors Cross like the Centre of Eternity is in Him, It taketh up his Thoughts, and exerciseth all the Powers of his soul, with Wonder Admiration Joy and Thanksgiving. The Omnipotence of God is his Hous, and Eternity his habitation.

Thomas Traherne, *Centuries*, I.54

The learning of charity, my brothers, its vigour, its flowers, its fruit, its beauty, its pleasantness, its sustenance, its drink, its food, its loving embraces – all these can never cloy. And if God grants us such delights upon our pilgrimage, what joys await us in our homeland!

St Augustine, *Homilies on I John*, 10.7

Blessed are the poor in spirit, for theirs is the Kingdom of heaven.

Blessed are those who mourn, for they shall be comforted.

Blessed are the meek, for they shall inherit the earth.

Blessed are they who hunger and thirst for righteousness, for they shall be satisfied.

Blessed are the merciful, for they shall obtain mercy.

Blessed are the pure in heart, for they shall see God.

Blessed are the peacemakers, for they shall be called sons of God.

Blessed are those who are persecuted for righteousness' sake, for theirs is the kingdom of heaven.

The Gospel according to St Matthew 5.3–10

But, as it is written, 'What no eye has seen, nor ear heard, nor the heart of man conceived, what God has prepared for those who love him.'

St Paul's First Epistle to the Corinthians 2.9

O God, who hast prepared for them that love thee such good things as pass men's understanding: Pour into our hearts such love towards thee, that we, loving thee above all things, may obtain thy promises, which exceed all that we can desire; through Jesus Christ our Lord.

The Book of Common Prayer, Collect for the Sixth Sunday after Trinity

. . . for our courteous Lord wants us to be as friendly with him as the heart may conceive or the soul may desire. But be careful not to take this friendliness too casually, so that we neglect courtesy; for our Lord himself is supreme friendliness, and he is as courteous as he is friendly; for he is truly courteous. And he wants the blessed creatures who will be with him in heaven for ever to be like himself in all things. And to be perfectly like our Lord is our true salvation and our full bliss. And if we are uncertain how we can do all this, let us ask our Lord and he will teach us; for it is his pleasure and his glory. Blessed may he be!

Julian of Norwich, *Revelations of Divine Love*, Chapter 77

But what are your delights to be? *And they shall delight in abundance of peace*: Peace, your gold; peace, your silver; peace, your life; peace, your God. Peace will fulfil your every desire. For what is here gold cannot become your silver; what is wine cannot become your bread; your light cannot become your drink also. Your God shall become all in all to you. He will be your meat, that you hunger not; your drink, that you do not thirst; your enlightening, that you be not blind; your stay and support, that you do not falter. Himself whole and entire, He will possess you whole and entire. You will not feel cramped for space in possessing Him with whom you possess all else besides. You shall have all and He shall have all, because you and He shall be one. This complete whole will be His who possesses you. These are the (V.37) *remnants for the peaceable man*. We have been singing this verse; it occurs in the Psalm a good way further on, it is true, from what we are now discussing, but since we have chanted it, we may very well conclude with it. Only be full of confidence.

St Augustine, *Discourses on the Psalms*, 'Second Discourse on Psalm 36' (Book of Common Prayer, Psalm 37.11)

Will you, sometime, who have sought so long and seek
Still in the slowly darkening hunting ground,
Catch sight some ordinary month or week
Of that strange quarry you scarcely thought you sought –
Yourself, the gatherer gathered, the finder found,
The buyer, who would buy all, in bounty bought –
And perch in pride on the princely hand, at home,
And there, the long hunt over, rest and roam?

Edwin Muir, 'The Question'

So he told them this parable: 'What man of you, having a hundred sheep, if he has lost one of them, does not leave the ninety-nine in the wilderness, and go after the one which is lost, until he finds it? And when he has found it, he lays it on his shoulders, rejoicing. And when he comes home, he calls together his friends and his neighbours, saying to them, "Rejoice with me, for I have found my sheep which was lost." Just so, I tell you, there will be more joy in heaven over one sinner who repents than over ninety-nine righteous persons who need no repentance.'

The Gospel according to St Luke 15.4–7

It is in God's face, then, that we shall be hidden. Do you expect to hear me describe the hiding place of God's countenance? Cleanse your heart so that He Himself may enlighten you, that He whom you invoke may take possession of you. Be you His dwelling place and He will be your dwelling place: let Him abide in you and you will abide in Him. If you welcome Him into your heart during this life, He will welcome you with His face when life is ended.

St Augustine, *Discourses on the Psalms*, 'Fourth Discourse on Psalm 30'
(Psalm 31.22 in the Book of Common Prayer)

. . . and when I awake up after thy likeness, I shall be satisfied with it.

Psalm 17.16

Are not praises the very end for which the world was created?

Thomas Traherne, *Centuries*, III.82

Even here there was a sharp distinction between Barth's and Brunner's tastes. Brunner was devoted to Bach. There was 'nothing more heavenly beautiful than Bach's Double Violin Concerto'. Barth's retort was that though the angels would probably have to

play Bach on feast-days, when they were by themselves they would
without doubt play Mozart.

Vernon Sprockton, *Love and Marriage*, 'Preface', selections from Emil Brunner,
The Divine Imperative, p. 10 n. 7

O quanta qualia sunt illa sabbata,
Quae semper celebrant superna curia,
Quae fessis requies, quae merces fortibus,
Cum erit omnia Deus in omnibus!

Quis rex, quae curia, quale palatium,
Quae pax, quae requies, quod illud gaudium!
Hujus participes exponant gloriae,
Si, quantum sentiunt, possint exprimere.

Vere Jerusalem illic est civitas,
Cujus pax jugis est summa jucunditas,
Ubi non praevenit rem desiderium,
Nec desiderio minus est praemium.

Illic molestiis finitis omnibus
Securi cantica Sion cantabimus,
Et juges gratias de donis gratiae
Beata referet plebs tibi, Domine.

Illic ex sabbato succedit sabbatum,
Perpes laetitia sabbatizantium,
Nec innefabiles cessabunt jubili,
Quos decantabimus et nos et angeli.

Nostrum est interim mentem erigere
Et totis patriam votis appetere,
Et ad Jerusalem a Babylonia
Post longa regredi tandem exilia.

Rising

Perenni Domino perpes sit gloria,
Ex quo sunt, per quem sunt, in quo sunt omnia;
Ex quo sunt, Pater est, per quem sunt, Filius,
In quo sunt Patris et Filii Spiritus.

How great, how glorious those holy sabbath-days,
Joyfully kept in God's heavenly court.
What rest for weariness, what prize for steadfastness,
When God's perfection shall be all in all!

What king, what judgement-seat, what royal palace,
What peace, what restfulness, what celebration!
Let those who share in that glory recount it,
If what they feel, they can utter to us.

Truly that city is named Jerusalem,
Whose peace unfailing is utmost delightfulness,
No more is wishing let down by reality,
Nor persists longing, unmet by reward.

There, where our troubles are over and finished,
Safely the anthems of Sion we'll sing,
O Lord, thy people, in endless gratefulness,
Offering back to thee thy gifts of grace.

There, now that sabbath-day follows on sabbath-day,
With joy perpetual keeping the festival,
Never shall die away those wordless jubilees,
Chanted for ever, by us and the angels.

Our part for now is to lift up our spirits,
Seeking our homeland with whole-hearted hungering
And to Jerusalem from Babylonia
After long exile at last now returning.

Now may the Lord be unceasingly glorified,
From whom and by whom and in whom are all things;
From whom, the Father and by whom, his only Son,
In whom, the Spirit, from Father and Son.

Peter Abelard; translated with help from Donald Whitton

Brethren, what we are to see is a vision, that neither eye hath seen nor ear hath heard nor hath come up into the heart of man – a vision surpassing all earthly beauties, of gold or silver, of woods or fields, the beauty of sea and sky, of sun, moon and stars, the beauty of angels: excelling all these things, for all have their beauty from him.

I said once before: Empty out that vessel that is to be filled; you are to be filled with good, pour away the evil. God would fill you, shall we say, with honey: where can you put it, if you are full of vinegar? What your vessel held must be poured away, and the vessel cleansed: cleansed, were it with toil and chafing, so that it be fit to hold – did we say honey? Gold? Wine? Speak as we may of that which cannot be spoken, call it what we will, its proper name is – God.

St Augustine, *Homilies on 1 John*, 4.5, 6

For the perfection of human nature consists perhaps in its very growth in goodness.

St Gregory of Nyssa, *The Life of Moses*, Prologue 10

There we shall be still and see; we shall see and we shall love; we shall love and we shall praise. Behold what will be, in the end, and not end! For what is our end but to reach that kingdom which has no end?

St Augustine, *The City of God*, XXII.30

Rising

... and I will give him the morning star.

Revelation 2.28

Prayer, the Church's banquet, Angel's age,
God's breath in man returning to his birth,
The soul in paraphrase, heart in pilgrimage,
The Christian plummet, sounding heaven and earth;
Engine against the Almighty, sinner's tower,
Reversèd thunder, Christ-side-piercing spear,
The six-days' world transposing in an hour,
A kind of tune, which all things hear and fear;
Softness, and peace, and joy, and love, and bliss,
Exalted manna, gladness of the best,
Heaven in ordinary, man well drest,
The milky way, the bird of Paradise,
Church-bells beyond the stars held, the soul's blood,
The land of spices, something understood.

George Herbert

With men it is impossible, but not with God; for all things are
possible with God.

The Gospel according to St Mark 10.27

The end of man is to glorify God and enjoy Him for ever.

The Shorter Catechism

O praise God in his holiness: praise him in the firmament of his
  power.
Praise him in his noble acts: praise him according to his excellent
  greatness.

Praise him in the sound of the trumpet: praise him in the lute and
  harp.
Praise him in the cymbals and dances: praise him upon the strings
  and pipe.
Praise him upon the well-tuned cymbals: praise him upon the loud
  cymbals.
Let everything that hath breath: praise the Lord.

Psalm 150

Acknowledgements

We would like to thank all those who have given us permission to repro-
duce extracts from publications in this book, as indicated in the list below.
Every effort has been made to trace copyright ownership. The publisher
would be grateful to be informed of any omissions.

Auden, W. H., 'Stop All The Clocks', copyright 1940 & renewed 1968 by
   W.H. Auden., from W.H. AUDEN: THE COLLECTED POEMS by
   W.H. Auden. Used by permission of Faber and Faber Ltd. (UK) and
   Random House, Inc (US).
Augustine, St, *Confessions*, translated by A. C. Outler, Library of Christian
   Classics, vol. VII, 1955, SCM Press (UK) and Westminster Press (US),
   permission sought.
   — translated by R. S. Pine-Coffin, 1961, Penguin Classics, permission
   sought.
   — translated by Henry Chadwick, 1991, Oxford University Press,
   permission sought.
Augustine, St, *Homilies on I John* and *The Trinity*, translated by John
   Burnaby, Library of Christian Classics, vol. VIII, 1955, SCM Press (UK)
   and Westminster Press (US), permission sought.
Augustine, St, *Discourses on the Psalms*, vol. II, translated Dame
   Scholastica Hebgin and Dame Felicitas Corrigan, 1961, Ancient
   Christian Writers, Westminster, Maryland: Newman Press, per-
   mission sought.
Augustine, St, *The City of God*, 1972, Pelican Classics, Penguin,
   permission sought.
Baker, John Austin, *The Foolishness of God* (London: Darton, Longman &
   Todd Ltd © 1970).
Barr, James, *The Bible in the Modern World* (London: SCM Press, 1973).
Betjeman, John, 'Christmas', *Collected Poems* (London: John Murray
   (Publishers) Ltd.).

Bloom, Anthony, *God and Man* (London: Darton, Longman & Todd Ltd © 1971).

Bloom, Anthony, *Living Prayer* (London: Darton, Longman & Todd Ltd © 1966).

Bloom, Anthony, *School for Prayer* (London: Darton, Longman & Todd Ltd © 1970).

Calvin, John, *Institutes of the Christian Religion* (Cambridge: James Clarke & Co.).

Chauduri, Nirad C., *Scholar Extraordinary: the life of Professor the Rt Hon Friedrich Max Müller PC* published by Chatto & Windus. Reprinted by permission of The Random House Group Ltd.

Dix, Dom Gregory, *The Shape of the Liturgy* (London and New York: Continuum).

Dunstan, G. R., *The Family Is Not Broken* (London: SCM Press, 1962).

Eliot, T. S., *The Cocktail Party* (London: Faber and Faber Ltd. and New York: Harcourt Brace & Company).

Eliot, T. S. *Four Quartets* (London: Faber and Faber Ltd. and New York: Harcourt Brace & Company).

Eliot, T. S., 'Journey of the Magi' (London: Faber and Faber Ltd. and New York: Harcourt Brace & Company).

Eliot, T. S., *Little Gidding* (London: Faber and Faber Ltd. and New York: Harcourt Brace & Company).

Eliot, T. S., 'Mr Eliot's Sunday morning service' (London: Faber and Faber Ltd. and New York: Harcourt Brace & Company).

Eliot, T. S., 'The Rock' (London: Faber and Faber Ltd. and New York: Harcourt Brace & Company).

Farrer, Austin, *A Celebration of Faith*. Reproduced by permission of Hodder and Stoughton Limited.

Farrer, Austin, *The Glass of Vision* (London: A&C Black, 1948).

Farrer, Austin, *Saving Belief*. Reproduced by permission of Hodder and Stoughton Ltd.

Gombrich, Ernst, *The Story of Art*. Reproduced from The Story of Art by E.H. Gombrich, 16th Edition © Phaidon Press Ltd, Text © E.H. Gombrich.

Gowers, Ernest, *The Complete Plain Words* (Reproduced by permission of The Stationery Office from *Complete Plain Words*, by Sir Ernest Gowers).

Hailsham, Lord, *The Door Wherein I Went* (London: HarperCollins Publishers Ltd, 1975)

Acknowledgements

Haldane, J. B. S., 'The Creator, if He exists, has a special preference for beetles' © the British Interplanetary Society, *JBIS* Vol. 10 No. 4, p. 156.

Hooker, Morna, *The Gospel according to St Mark* (London and New York: Continuum).

Housman, A. E., 'Easter Hymn' (Reprinted by permission of The Society of Authors as the Literary Representative of the Estate of A. E. Housman), from THE COLLECTED POEMS OF A. E. HOUSMAN Copyright 1936 by Barclays Bank Ltd., © 1964 by Robert E. Symons. Reprinted by permission of Henry Holt and Company, LLC.

Jenkins, David E., *God, Jesus and Life in the Spirit* (London: SCM Press, 1988).

Jenkins, David E., *What Is Man?* (London: SCM Press, 1970).

Julian of Norwich, *Revelations of Divine Love* by Julian of Norwich, translated by Elizabeth Spearing (Penguin Classics, 1998) translation copyright © Elizabeth Spearing, 1998.

Keynes, John Maynard, *The General Theory of Employment, Interest and Money* (The Collected Writings of John Maynard Keynes, Elisabeth Johnson and Donald Moggridge, vol. 7; Cambridge: Cambridge University Press, 1978).

Kipling, Rudyard, 'The Appeal' (Reproduced by permission of A. P. Watt Ltd on behalf of The National Trust for Places of Historical Interest or Natural Beauty).

Kipling, Rudyard, 'McAndrew's Hymn' (Reproduced by permission of A.P. Watt Ltd on behalf of The National Trust for Places of Historical Interest or Natural Beauty).

Kipling, Rudyard, 'Sussex' (Reproduced by permission of A.P. Watt Ltd on behalf of The National Trust for Places of Historical Interest or Natural Beauty).

Lewis, C. S., GEORGE MACDONALD AN ANTHOLOGY © C.S. Lewis Pte. Ltd. 1947. Extracts reprinted by permission.

Lewis, C. S., MERE CHRISTIANITY © C.S. Lewis Pte. Ltd. 1942, 1943, 1944, 1952. Extracts reprinted by permission.

Lewis, C. S., *Out of the Silent Planet* published by Bodley Head. Reprinted by permission of The Random House Group Ltd.

Lewis, C. S., THE SCREWTAPE LETTERS © C.S. Lewis Pte. Ltd. 1942. Extracts reprinted by permission.

Lorenz, Konrad, *On Aggression* (London: Routledge).

Lovejoy, Arthur O., *The Great Chain of Being* (Reprinted by permission of the publisher from THE GREAT CHAIN OF BEING: A STUDY OF

THE HISTORY OF AN IDEA by Arthur O. Lovejoy, Cambridge, Mass.: Harvard University Press, Copyright © 1936, 1964 by the President and Fellows of Harvard College).

MacNeice, Louis, 'A Fanfare for the Makers' (London: David Higham Associates Limited).

Masefield, John, 'The Everlasting Mercy' (Reprinted by permission of The Society of Authors as the Literary Representative of the Estate of John Masefield).

Midgley, Mary, *Beast and Man* (Harlow: Pearson Education Limited).

Muir, Edwin, 'One foot in Eden', 'The Question', 'Milton', 'The Animals', from *Variations on a Time Theme*, from 'Prometheus', and from 'The Transfiguration', in *Collected poems 1921–1958*. Used by permission of Faber & Faber Ltd. (UK) and Oxford University Press Inc. (US) © 1960 by Willa Muir.

Murdoch, Iris, *The Sovereignty of Good* (London: Routledge).

Nash, Ogden, 'A caution to everyone' is used with kind permission of André Deutsch Ltd. 2001. Reprinted by permission of Curtis Brown, Ltd.

Nash, Ogden, 'The shrimp' taken from 'Candy is Dandy' is used with kind permission of André Deutsch Ltd. 2001. Reprinted by permission of Curtis Brown, Ltd.

Norton, Lucy, *Historical Memoirs of the Duc of Saint-Simon: A Shortened Version*, Vol. 2, p. 128 (Reproduced by permission of the Estate of Lucy Norton).

Otto, Rudolf, *The Idea of the Holy* (translated by John Harvey; second edition, 1950)(Reprinted by permission of Oxford University Press).

Price, H. H., 'Clarity is not enough' (Reprinted by courtesy of the Editor of the Aristotelian Society: © 1945).

Sayers, Dorothy L., *Murder Must Advertise* (London: Hodder Headline). Used by permission of David Higham Associates Limited.

Sayers, Dorothy L., *The Nine Tailors* (London: Hodder Headline). Used by permission of David Higham Associates Limited.

Sellar, W. C. and R. J. Yeatman, *1066 and All That* (London: Methuen Publishing Limited).

Vanstone, W. H., *Love's Endeavour, Love's Expense* (London: Darton, Longman & Todd Ltd).

Williams, Charles, *The English Poetic Mind* (Oxford: Oxford University Press).

Woolf, Virginia, *Flush* (Reprinted by permission of The Society of Authors as the Literary Representative of the Estate of John and Virginia Woolf).

Acknowledgements

Yeats, W. B., 'He Wishes for the Cloths of Heaven' (Reprinted by permission of Michael Yeats).

Yeats, W. B., 'The Second Coming' (Reprinted by permission of Michael Yeats).

Bibliographic Information

Abelard, Peter, 'O quanta qualia', No. 349 in *The Oxford Hymn Book* (Oxford: Oxford University Press, 1908).

Addison, Joseph, 'The spacious firmament on high', in Arthur Quiller-Couch (ed.), *The Oxford Book of English Verse*, new edn (Oxford: Clarendon Press, 1939).

Anonymous, 'Great Chatham with his sabre drawn', in *Oxford Dictionary of Quotations*, 5th edn (Oxford: Oxford University Press, 1999).

——, 'A Lyke-Wake dirge', in Arthur Quiller-Couch (ed.), *The Oxford Book of English Verse*, new edn (Oxford: Clarendon Press, Oxford, 1939), pp. 451–2.

——, 'Post tenebras spero lucem', on a tombstone in the church of Santa Maria del Popolo, Rome.

——, 'The dream of the Rood', in Helen Gardner (ed.), *The Faber Book of Religious Verse* (London: Faber & Faber, 1972), pp. 25–9.

——, 'Tam Lin', in Arthur Quiller-Couch (ed.), *The Oxford book of English Verse*, new edition (Oxford: Clarendon Press, 1939), pp. 418–28.

——, 'When in Rome, do as the Romans do' (proverb).

Aristotle, *Ethics*, Everyman's Library (London: Dent, London, 1970), p. 186.

Arnold, Matthew, *Poems* (London: Oxford University Press, 1942).

Auden, W. H., 'Stop all the clocks', *Collected Poems* (London: Faber & Faber, 1991).

Augustine, St, *The City of God*, Pelican Classics (Harmondsworth: Penguin, 1972).

——, *Confessions*, Library of Christian Classics, Vol. VII, trans. A. C. Outler (London: SCM Press, and Philadelphia: Westminster Press, 1955).

——, *Confessions*, Penguin Classics, trans. R. S. Pine-Coffin (Harmondsworth: Penguin, 1961).

——, *Confessions*, trans. Henry Chadwick (Oxford: Oxford University Press, 1991).

——, *Homilies on 1 John and The Trinity*, Library of Christian Classics, Vol. VIII, trans. John Burnaby (London: SCM Press, and Philadelphia: Westminster Press, 1955).

——, *Discourses on the Psalms*, Vol. II, Ancient Christian Writers, trans. Dame Scholastica Hebgin and Dame Felicitas Corrigan (Westminster, Maryland: Newman Press, 1961).

Austen, Jane, *Mansfield Park*, The Penguin English Library (Harmondsworth: Penguin, 1966).

——, *Northanger Abbey*, The Penguin English Library (Harmondsworth: Penguin, 1972).

——, *Pride and Prejudice*, Penguin Classics (London: Penguin, 1996).

——, *Sense and Sensibility*, The Penguin English Library (Harmondsworth: Penguin, 1969).

——, epitaph, in Winchester Cathedral.

Baker, John Austin, *The Foolishness of God* (London: Darton, Longman & Todd, 1970).

Barr, James, *The Bible in the Modern World* (London: SCM Press, 1973).

Baxter, Richard, *The Christian Directory* in Waldo Beach and H. Richard Niebuhr (eds), Chapter 10, 'Ethics of Puritanism and Quakerism', *Christian Ethics: Sources of the Living Tradition* (New York: Ronald, 1955), pp. 313–14.

Bede, The Venerable, inscription in Durham Cathedral.

Bentham, Jeremy, *Introduction to the Principles of Morals and Legislation* (Oxford: Clarendon Press, 1996), Chapter 17 (footnote).

Betjeman, John, *Collected Poems* (London: John Murray, 1979).

Bible: King James Version (Oxford University Press).

——, Revised Standard Version (London: Thomas Nelson & Sons, 1959).

Blake, William, *Poetical Works* (London: Oxford University Press, 1913, reprinted 1948).

Bloom, Anthony, *God and Man* (London: Darton, Longman & Todd, 1971).

——, *Living Prayer* (London: Darton, Longman & Todd, Libra Books, 1966).

——, *School for Prayer* (London: Darton, Longman & Todd, Libra Books, 1970).

Brevint, Daniel, *The Christian sacrament, and sacrifice* (Oxford, 1673).

Browning, Robert, *Poems*, 2 vols, Penguin English Poets (Harmondsworth: Penguin, 1981).

Burns, Robert, *The Poems and Songs*, Collins Classics (Glasgow: Collins, 1976).

Butler, Joseph, Bishop, *Fifteen sermons preached at the Rolls Chapel*, Preface, *Works*, ed. Gladstone (Oxford: Clarendon Press, 1896), Vol. II.

——, Letter to John Wesley, 16 August 1739, Wesley's *Journal*, in *Oxford Dictionary of Quotations*, 5th edn (Oxford: Oxford University Press, 1999).

Butler, Samuel, *Hudibras* (1663), English Texts (Oxford: Clarendon Press, 1973).

Byron, Lord, *Complete Poetical Works* (Oxford: Clarendon Press, 1993).

Callimachus, 'Epigram 1', tr. William Cory, in Arthur Quiller-Couch (ed.), *The Oxford Book of English Verse*, new edn (Oxford: Clarendon Press, 1939). Adapted by Ivo Mosley.

Calvin, John, *Institutes of the Christian Religion*, in Waldo Beach and H. Richard Niebuhr (eds), *Christian Ethics: Sources of the Living Tradition* (New York: Ronald, 1955), Chapter 9.

Chaucer, Geoffrey, 'The Knight's Tale', *The Canterbury Tales* (Oxford: Oxford University Press, 1985).

Chauduri, Nirad C., *Scholar Extraordinary: The Life of Professor the Rt Hon. Friedrich Max Müller, PC* (London: Chatto & Windus, 1974).

Clough, Arthur Hugh, *Poems* (Oxford: Oxford University Press, 1986).

Clutton Brock, A., 'A dream of heaven', in *Immortality* (London: Macmillan, 1917).

Coleridge, Samuel Taylor, *Poems* (London: Oxford University Press, reprinted 1940).

Common Prayer, Book of, Oxford University Press.

Cory, William, 'Minnermus in church', in Helen Gardner (ed.), *The New Oxford Book of English Verse*, (Oxford: Clarendon Press, 1972).

——, *see* Callimachus.

Cotton, Charles, 'Evening quatrains' (1689).

Cowper, William, *Poems* (Oxford: Clarendon Press, 1980).

Dante Alighieri, *Purgatorio*, Temple Classics (London: J. M. Dent, 1901).

Dante Alighieri, *Paradiso*, Temple Classics (London: J. M. Dent, 1899).

Dix, Gregory, *The Shape of the Liturgy* (Westminster: Dacre Press, 1945).

Donne, John, *Complete English Poems* (Harmondsworth: Penguin, 1982).

Dryden, John, 'A song for St Cecilia's Day 1687', in Arthur Quiller-Couch (ed.), *The Oxford Book of English Verse*, new edn (Oxford: Clarendon Press, 1939).

Dunbar, William, 'Lament for the makers', *Poems* (Oxford: Clarendon Press, 1979).

Dunstan, G. R., *The Family Is Not Broken* (London: SCM Press, 1962).

Eastern Church, a prayer of, in Frank Colquhoun (ed.), *Parish Prayers* (London: Hodder & Stoughton, 1967).

Eliot, T. S., *Complete Poems and Plays* (London: Faber & Faber, 1969).

Elizabeth I, *The Oxford Dictionary of Quotations* (1999) says that this was her answer, on being asked her opinion of Christ's presence in the Eucharist; and refers to S. Clarke *The marrow of ecclesiastical history* (1675).

Exeter Cathedral, epitaph in.

Farrer, A. M., *A Celebration of Faith* (London: Hodder & Stoughton, 1970).

——, *The Glass of Vision*, Bampton Lectures for 1948 (Westminster: Dacre Press, 1948).

——, *Saving Belief* (London: Hodder & Stoughton, 1964).

——, *A Science of God?* (London: Bles, 1966).

Flecker, James Elroy, 'The Gates of Damascus', *Collected Poems* (London: Secker & Warburg, 1946).

Fox, Caroline, *Memories of Old Friends* (Philadelphia: Lippincott, 1882), quoted in Howard H. Brinton, *Quaker Journals: Varieties of Religious Experience among Friends* (Wallingford, Pennsylvania: Pendle Hill Publications, 1972).

Gelasian Sacramentary, a prayer from, in Frank Colquhoun (ed.), *Parish Prayers* (London: Hodder & Stoughton, 1967).

Goethe, Johann Wolfgang von, *Faust*, 'Prolog im Himmel' and Part 1 (Hamburg: Christian Wegner Verlag, 1968).

——, 'Mignons Lied', in *Das Oxforder Buch Deutscher Dichtung* (Oxford: Oxford University Press, 1915).

Gombrich, E. H., *The Story of Art*, 16th edn (London: Phaidon Press, revised, expanded and redesigned 1995).

Gowers, Ernest, *The Complete Plain Words* (London: Her Majesty's Stationery Office, 1954, revised edition, 1973).

Gregory of Nyssa, *The Life of Moses*, The Classics of Western Spirituality (New York: Paulist Press, 1978).

Hailsham, Lord, *The Door Wherein I Went* (London: Collins, 1975).

Haldane, J. B. S., in a lecture given on 7 April 1951, printed in the *Journal of the British Interplanetary Society*, Vol. 10.

Hare, Kenneth, *Poems* (London: Ernest Benn, 1923).

Hebrew grace, see Lawrence A. Hoffman, 'Rabbinic *Berakhah* and Jewish Spirituality', in Christian Duquoc and Casiano Florestan (eds), *Asking and Thanking* (London: Concilium and SCM Press, 1990), pp. 19 and 23.

Hebrew wedding blessing, part of the Seven Blessings recited at a Jewish wedding.

Herbert, George, *Works* (Oxford: Clarendon Press, 1941.

Herrick, Robert, 'To keep a true Lent', Oxford Standard Authors (London: Oxford University Press, 1971).

Homer, *Odyssey*, Book 15, line 84.

Hooker, Morna, *The Gospel according to St Mark*, Black's New Testament Commentaries (London: Black, 1991).

Hopkins, Gerard Manley, 'God's grandeur', *The Complete Poems, with Selected Prose* (London: Fount, 1996).

Housman, A. E., 'Easter hymn', *Collected Poems and Selected Prose* (Harmondsworth: Penguin, 1989).

Hume, David, *Dialogues concerning Natural Religion*, ed. Norman Kemp Smith, 2nd edn (London: Thomas Nelson & Sons, 1947).

Jenkins, Claude, in a sermon at Christ Church, Oxford, *c.* 1955.

Jenkins, David, *What Is Man?*, Centrebooks (London: SCM Press, 1970).

——, *God, Jesus and Life in the Spirit* (London: SCM Press, 1988).

Jones, William, epigram, in Arthur Quiller-Couch (ed.), *The Oxford Book of English Verse*, new edn (Oxford: Clarendon Press, 1939).

Jonson, Ben, 'Her triumph', *Works*, Vol. VIII, *The Poems: the Prose Works* (Oxford: Clarendon Press, 1947).

Julian of Norwich, *Revelations of Divine Love*, Penguin Classics (London: Penguin, 1998).

Kant, Immanuel, *Critique of Practical Reason* (Cambridge: Cambridge University Press, 1997).

Keats, John, *Poems*, Annotated English Poets (London: Longman, 1970).

——, *Letters*, ed. M. B. Forman, 2nd edn (Oxford: Oxford University Press, 1935).

Keynes, J. M., *General Theory of Employment, Interest and Money*, 'Preface', *Collected Writings*, Vol. 7 (London: Macmillan, 1974).

Kipling, Rudyard, *The Definitive Edition of Rudyard Kipling's Verse* (London: Hodder & Stoughton, 1940).

Küng, Hans, *The Council and Reunion* (London and New York: Sheed & Ward, 1961).

Lamb, Charles, *Essays of Elia*, World's Classics (Oxford: Oxford University Press, 1987).

——, Letter to William Wordsworth, 20 March 1822, *Works of Charles and Mary Lamb, Letters*, Vol. 7 (London: Methuen, 1905).

Lewis, C. S., *The Screwtape Letters* (1942), republished in *The Screwtape Letters and Screwtape Proposes a Toast* (London: Bles, 1961).

——, *Mere Christianity* (London: Bles, 1952).

——, *Out of the Silent Planet* (London: Bodley Head, 1938).

——, George MacDonald, *Anthology*, ed. C. S. Lewis (London: Bles, 1946).

Lorenz, Konrad, *On Aggression* (London: Methuen, 1966).

Lovejoy, Arthur O., *The Great Chain of Being* (Harvard University Press, 1953).

Lucia, Santa, epitaph, on the church of S. Geremia in Venice.

Luther, Martin, quoted in G. Rupp, *The Righteousness of God* (London: Hodder & Stoughton, 1953), p. 314.

Macaulay, T. B., Lord, *Works* (London: Longmans, Green & Co., 1875), Vol. I, *History of England*; Vol. VIII, *Lays of Ancient Rome*, 'Horatius'.

MacDonald, George, *Anthology*, ed. C. S. Lewis (London: Bles, 1946).

MacNeice, Louis, 'A Fanfare for the Makers', *Collected Poems* (London: Faber & Faber, 1966).

Marlowe, Christopher, *Doctor Faustus, Complete Works*, Vol. 2, Oxford English Texts (Oxford: Clarendon Press, 1990).

Marvell, Andrew, in Arthur Quiller-Couch (ed.), *The Oxford Book of English Verse*, new edn (Oxford: Clarendon Press, 1939).

Masefield, John, 'The Everlasting Mercy', *Complete Works* (London: Heinemann, 1932).

Metropolitan Museum, New York: on an oriental painting of finches 1254–1302.

Mevlana, founder of the whirling dervishes (thirteenth century), inscription at his shrine in Konya, Turkey.

Meynell, Alice, 'Christ in the universe', in Helen Gardner (ed.), *The Faber Book of Religious Verse* (London: Faber & Faber, 1972, pp. 25–9).

Meyer, Kuno, *see* 'St Patrick's Breastplate'.

Midgley, Mary, *Beast and Man: The Roots of Human Nature* (Hassocks: Harvester Press, 1978).

Milton, John, *Areopagitica* (1644), Everyman's Library (London: Dent, 1990).

——, *Poetical Works* (London: Oxford University Press, 1904).

Muir, Edwin, *An Autobiography* (London: Hogarth Press, 1954).

——, *Collected Poems* 1921–58 (London: Faber & Faber, 1960).

Müller, Max, *see* Chauduri, Nirad C.

Murdoch, Iris, *The Sovereignty of Good* (London: Routledge & Kegan Paul, 1970).

Nash, Ogden, 'Fellow Creatures: The Shrimp', *Everyone But Thee and Me* (London: Dent, 1963).

Nesbit, E., *The Magic City* (London: Benn, 1910).

Newbolt, Henry, 'He fell among thieves', in Arthur Quiller-Couch (ed.), *The Oxford Book of English Verse*, new edn (Oxford: Clarendon Press, 1939).

Oppenheimer, Helen, 'Holy sepulchre', previously unpublished.

Otto, Rudolf, *The Idea of the Holy*, trans. John W. Harvey, 2nd edn (London: Oxford University Press, 1950).

Owen, Wilfred, 'Anthem for doomed youth', in Helen Gardner (ed.), *The New Oxford Book of English Verse* (Oxford: Clarendon Press, 1972).

Oxyrhynchus Papyri. See entry in F. L. Cross and E. A. Livingstone (eds), *The Oxford Dictionary of the Christian Church*, 3rd edn (Oxford: Oxford University Press, 1997).

'St Patrick's Breastplate', trans. Kuno Meyer, in *Selections from Ancient Irish Poetry*, 2nd edn (Constable, 1913), quoted in John V. Taylor, *The Primal Vision* (London: SCM Press, 1963).

Platen, August Graf von, 'Venedig', in *Das Oxforder Buch Deutscher Dichtung* (Oxford: Oxford University Press, 1915).

Pope, Alexander, 'An Essay on Man', *The Poems of Alexander Pope*, Vol. III, ed. Maynard Mack (London: Methuen, 1950).

Price, H. H., 'Clarity is not enough', Presidential address delivered at the Joint Session of the Mind Association and the Aristotelian Society 1945, published in H. D. Lewis (ed.), *Clarity Is Not Enough* (London: Allen & Unwin, 1963).

Psalms, Book of Common Prayer (Oxford University Press).

Roman Missal, 'Exsultet' on Holy Saturday.

Saint Simon, Duke of, *Historical Memoirs 1710–1715*, trans. Lucy Norton (London: Hamish Hamilton, 1967).

Saki, 'The Lumber Room', *Short Stories: Beasts and Super-beasts* (John Lane: The Bodley Head, 1930).

Sayers, Dorothy L., *Murder Must Advertise* (London: Victor Gollancz, 1933).

——, *The Nine Tailors* (London: Victor Gollancz, 1934).

Sellar, W. C., and R. J. Yeatman, *1066 and All That*, Fontana Library (London: Methuen, 1930).

Shakespeare, William, 3 vols, ed. Edward Dowden (London: Oxford University Press, 1912).

Shelley, Percy Bysshe, *Complete Poetical Works* (London: Oxford University Press, 1947 (1934)).

Shirley, James, 'Death the leveller', in *The contention of Ajax and Ulysses* (1659), in Arthur Quiller-Couch (ed.), *The Oxford Book of English Verse*, new edn (Oxford: Clarendon Press, 1939).

Shorter Catechism, drawn up by the Westminster Assembly, 1647.

Sidney, Philip, 'Loving in truth', *Astrophil & Stella* (1591), sonnet 1.

Southey, Robert, 'After Blenheim', in Palgrave's *Golden Treasury* (London: Macmillan, 1890).

Sprockton, Vernon, *Love and Marriage*, selections from Emil Brunner, *The Divine Imperative* (Collins Fontana, 1970).

Stevenson, R. L., *Travels with a Donkey in the Cevennes*, *Works* (26 vols), Vol. 1 (London: Heinemann, 1922).

Tennyson, Alfred, Lord, *Poems* (3 vols), ed. C. Ricks (Longmans, 1987).

Thackeray, William Makepeace, *Vanity Fair* (London: Pan Books, 1980).

Thompson, Francis, 'To a poet, breaking silence', *Collected Poems* (London: Burns & Oates, 1913).

Traherne, Thomas, *Centuries, Poems, & Thanksgivings*, 2 vols (Oxford: Clarendon Press, 1958).

University of Oxford, bidding prayer used at university sermons.

Vanstone, W. H., *Love's Endeavour Love's Expense* (London: Darton, Longman & Todd, 1977).

Veen, Johan Van, *Dredge Drain Reclaim*, 5th edn (Netherlands: Martinus Nijhoff, 1962).

Vespasian: Suetonius, *Lives of the Caesars*, section 23, subsect. 4.

Voltaire, *Dictionnaire Philosophique: Art Dramatique* (1764).

Wesley, Charles, 'Wrestling Jacob', in Arthur Quiller-Couch (ed.), *The Oxford Book of English Verse*, new edn (Oxford: Clarendon Press, 1939).

Wickremesinghe, Lakshman, used at a meeting of the Inter-Anglican Theological and Doctrinal Commission which met from 1981 to 1985.

Wilde, Oscar, *An Ideal Husband* (1895), *Works* (London: Collins).

Williams, Charles, *The English Poetic Mind* (Oxford: Clarendon Press, 1932).

Woolf, Virginia, *Flush: A Biography* (London: Hogarth Press, 1958).

Wordsworth, William, *Poetical Works* (6 vols)(Oxford: Oxford University Press, 1949).

Wordsworth, William and Dorothy Wordsworth, *Letters of William & Dorothy Wordsworth* (Oxford: Clarendon Press, 1935).

Wotton, Henry, 'Upon the death of Sir Albert Morton's wife', in Arthur Quiller-Couch (ed.), *The Oxford Book of English Verse*, new edn (Oxford: Clarendon Press, 1939).

Wren, Christopher, epitaph, in St Paul's Cathedral.

Yeats, W. B., 'Aedh wishes for the cloths of heaven', *Collected Poems* (London: Arena, 1990).

——, 'The Second Coming', *Collected Poems* (London: Arena, 1990).

Index of Authors and Sources

Where an author is referred to by another the entry is in parentheses.